To Thor
The coolest, most loving, arrogant cat in the world. I miss you
every day.

I'll Tell You What I Think

Kelly Thacker

Published by Kelly Thacker, 2023.

While every precaution has been taken in the preparation of this book, the publisher assumes no responsibility for errors or omissions, or for damages resulting from the use of the information contained herein.

I'LL TELL YOU WHAT I THINK

First edition. September 11, 2023.

Prologue

I'm falling through space. It is black, a darkness so complete, it's impossible to establish what is in front or below me, blocking my reflexes from any ability to navigate away from danger. I must be in a raging tornado because I can feel wet items slapping and entwining themselves about me. I land on a ledge and try to grasp a surface to hold onto, but the surface is smooth and nothing exists to secure my footing. And this fall has not been feet first as I am used to managing when falling from a great height.

Then I rotate in the darkness and fall again, only to land back on the same smooth surface and reach out desperately, grasping for anything to somehow hold me in place. But there is nothing, no help, no one to reach out and grab me, to give me relief, to make this nightmare stop.

I hear a loud, continuous roar, like the deafening sound a car engine makes when standing too close. How long have I been here in this never-ending hell?

And then suddenly it is over. The roar has stopped, and I am no longer falling. I lay in an exhausted heap unable to open my eyes, hoping the torture is over.

A door opens and the darkness is flooded with light.

"Stupid cat," he says. *"How on earth did you get in there?"*

I hear the running of footsteps. *"Honey, what was that sound? I heard this thump, thump and the cat crying. What did you do to him?"*

"I didn't do anything to him. He must have crawled into the dryer between loads, and when I turned it on, he was in there."

"How long was he in there? It sounded like forever."

"Only a few seconds. I was right here."

It may have only been a few seconds, but it felt like forever. Bleary-eyed, I stumble out of that chamber, drop onto the floor and affix The Master with an imposing glare. Stupid cat? How about stupid human? How did you fail to note my presence? Are you daft? I heave a frustrated sigh and shake my head at his ineptitude. *Oy vey*, I suppose I must learn to be more tolerant of the inferior human species. But not today. After that experience I need a stiff drink (more about that later) and a long nap.

Chapter One

The Beginning

I don't remember my mother. And I assume my father was a hit-and-run kind of guy, because no mention has ever been made of him. According to the Young Miss, she found me on the doorstep when I was about four weeks old, and how could she not have pity on such a helpless thing and bring him into their home to love and nurture?

The Master and Mrs. were out of town at my tender arrival, and although I was just beginning to get a grasp on the human language, I most definitely understood the yelling coming through the phone when the Young Miss tried her best to announce my presence.

"That cat better be gone when I get home!"

THAT CAT? First of all I was just a kitten, an infant, a babe-in-arms if you will, too young to even leave my mother. The Young Miss had immediately started me on formula, and I hadn't yet developed my epicurean palate where I could begin to dictate just what brands of cat food I would and would not eat. I had been snatched from the very jaws of death, that of being stuffed into a burlap bag and drowned, had I not been rescued. The mere thought makes me shudder. No wonder I'm so averse to water.

So there I was, *that cat*, wondering just what plans The Master had for me when he got home. Surely he couldn't be so heartless as to stuff me into the burlap bag himself and finish the job.

I could have worried about that fateful day when we would meet and a decision made, but I took full advantage of being totally adored and smothered with affection by the Young Miss. And, if the truth be told, I never gave it another thought. I am a cat after all - or *that cat* if you want to use the more particular vernacular of my precarious position at that time – and we are the masters of getting our way.

The Master and Mrs. did eventually arrive home, and I remember our first encounter well. I was in the kitchen licking formula out of a saucer. I had to have feedings at close intervals, so I have rather a collage of memories of endless saucers and much time in the kitchen that all seem to blur together. But I do remember the Mrs. falling head over heels in love on the spot.

"Oh look at him, he's so tiny! And how funny he looks when he eats, with that tiny little body and that long, long tail straight out behind him. I think he'll have to grow into his tail."

I ignored that rather rude comment and listened with my heart instead of my ears. Despite the none-too-flattering assessment of my tail, I heard pure unadulterated adoration and knew I just might have a chance at avoiding the burlap bag.

From The Master on the other hand, he issued forth much blustering and posturing. I had the keen sense of his delicate position. He had after all emphatically stated *that cat* had better be gone when he got home. And here I was, obviously, *not gone*.

I'LL TELL YOU WHAT I THINK

So what was he to do? Coo and trill in delight at my being not gone? Certainly not, he had a reputation at stake here. The Master conveyed both indifference and anger simultaneously. And I must say I was extremely impressed at the show he made of it too. He was downright awe-inspiring at how he managed to exhibit his complete disapproval of my presence while allowing the Young Miss to win if you will, and let me stay. For I noted the lesson to be learned at that moment – and I learned it well because I truly did want to avoid the burlap bag – there could only be one alpha male in the household, and it wasn't me.

No matter. As I previously said, I am a cat, and if there's one thing we are, it's intensely clever. I most certainly would be the alpha male, I simply wouldn't let The Master know I was and he wasn't. I could forego the official title of alpha male in this family if it meant the burlap bag could metaphorically be permanently burned or shredded, or better yet, stuffed with something heavy and drowned sans *that cat*.

Chapter Two

The Alpha Male

My name is Thor. The Young Miss had been into mythology and thought it would be suitable in light of my majestic black and white tuxedo coat. Yes, I could picture myself as the Norse God. She had to have had a sense that I needed a name as truly magnificent as my persona would later reflect. I think it fits me perfectly, and if I were to be truthful, I feel a little snobbish when I hear names given to others of my kind. Apparently one of my predecessors had the misfortune of being named Princess, then changed to Darla, then eventually just Kitty. A bad experimentation by the Young Miss in her youth. When considering what to name me, she actually bandied about several awkwardly inappropriate names such as Oreo and Scooter.

I've heard the Mrs. say I should have been named Socks because when I stand with my front paws perfectly aligned, I have two identical white socks. It really is quite striking in contrast to the jet black of the fur on the rest of my legs. But Socks as a name? I despair at such a thought.

I wasn't the only animal in the household. There was a feline named Juno (the Young Miss had really been on a roll with those mythological names) and Maggie the dog. I don't much like to talk about either one of them. Maggie, I still have a soft spot for her. More to come about her later, and then you'll understand why I don't talk about her much.

But Juno? Ugh. I mean—ugh, there really is nothing more to say. A nastier more unpleasant cat you'd be hard pressed to find. Her loyalties ran with the Young Miss and the Young Miss only. On a rare occasion, the Mrs. would have the good fortune to actually see her in the flesh and make an attempt to pet her. But she would be gone in a flash to where she was comfortable, under the Young Miss's bed. The Master claims he sometimes wondered if Young Miss even had another cat besides me because he never saw her. Yes, she was that antisocial. Not that I would have actually passed any companionable time with her, but she could have made some effort to at least be cordial. And maybe a little extended courtesy to welcome the new arrival.

And as the months went by, I hoped she would treat me as something other than persona non gratis and maybe come to appreciate my wonderful qualities too numerous to name. But no, it was not to be, for Juno remained continuously disagreeable.

So you can understand why I felt it imperative to finally establish myself as the alpha male around here and why it was necessary to scatter a little of my, how shall I say it? "scent" around the bedroom we shared. I hesitate to use a stronger word as I intend this memoir to be suitable for family reading, and I don't want to offend anyone's delicate sensibilities.

And so in thus scattering a little "scent" around, Juno would therefore clearly perceive who was in charge. All right, so maybe it was more than a little, especially when I wished to drive a particular point home about who got to sleep closest to Young Miss at night. Sometimes one is left with no choice but to leave a little "scent" on an entire pile of the Young Miss's newly laundered clothes. And maybe in all four corners of the bedroom. But that had been to establish boundaries when dealing with the unfriendly one. You really can't blame me. If you'd had to live with that unpleasant feline, I'm quite confident you'd agree with my subversive tactics.

As I've analyzed the entire scenario, I deduced a little jealousy on my part that Juno clearly held a special spot in Young Miss's heart, and I don't do well with second fiddle. Oh, don't get me wrong. If there was anything Young Miss loved, it was cats. In fact, I felt the Mrs. tended to overdo gifts with cat themes: pajamas, calendars, books (one in particular called *I Could Pee On This and Other Poems by Cats*. A rather vulgar title to my way of thinking. Surely a little consideration could have been given to family values as I have, and a more appropriate title might be *I Could "Scent" On This)*, T-shirts, and other various *objets d'art*. I often wondered if Young Miss secretly wished the cat-themed gifts would stop.

But although I knew Young Miss loved me dearly, I've never been able to stomach the idea of coming in second. And so I considered the transferring of my affections to other members of the household. I only had two choices, The Master or the Mrs. It couldn't be the Mrs. because her heart had clearly been given away long ago to Maggie the dog. Yes, I knew she loved me, she just didn't love me as much. How do I know, you ask? Why, I heard it from her very lips. She actually had the audacity - and extremely bad taste I might add - to say to Maggie, "*I love you best.*"

Once again, second fiddle just would not do. And so that left me with The Master. Yes, he had called me *that cat,* but I must say I love a good challenge. There was that nonsense about his being allergic, but that had surely been a ruse to keep up his ridiculous pretense of not liking me. Trying to maintain alpha male status requires diligence, so I recognized his declaration of being allergic to cats as just that, a ruse.

Now how to go about it. I knew it would require some finesse on my part. I couldn't just charge up to him and jump into his arms. Or could I? Actually, as I contemplated the situation, I decided a little boldness might be appreciated. This could give me a chance to demonstrate I had been taking careful notes on how to act like an alpha male.

And let me tell you, I did just that. I found The Master at his desk one day, his fingers busily typing at the keyboard, and I knew my chance had come. Without so much as a by-your-leave, I jumped up on his desk startling him momentarily, which forced him to stop and turn his full attention on me. A good move, I decided. I might want to use my newly discovered "jump and startle" tactic whenever I wanted his undivided attention. (Which, I suspected, would be often.)

I then marched directly onto the computer keyboard and pranced back and forth. And I must say I certainly enjoyed this new sensation. I actually liked the feel of those keys; they might come in handy for a bit of a foot massage. Xxxxxxxxxxxxxxxxxxxxxxxxx, ttttttttttttttttttttt, mmmmmmm, ppppppppppppppppppp.

"Thor! Get down!"

I'LL TELL YOU WHAT I THINK

Then The Master scooped me up and tossed me off the desk like so much dirty laundry. But never you mind, persistence, that's the stuff. Back up I jumped and sat down firmly, this time directly on the keys.

"*Move!*"

More scooping, and I found myself back on the floor again.

This was proving to be more difficult than I at first thought. Surely my very presence should be seen as a great compliment. Was he so daft as to miss my not-so-subtle signal that I was willing to be the center of his universe? I fluffed my fur in a firm resolve and got ready to commence battle.

Up, down, up, down, then time for drastic measures on his part as he threw me out of the room and slammed the door.

I couldn't believe my good fortune. Didn't he know about cats and closed doors? I flexed my paws and really got to work. Pow, pow, pow, I tapped in syncopated rhythm against the door.

"*Thor!*" shouted an angry voice from the other side.

Pow, pow, pow, pow, pow, pow. Ah, this was so delightful, I could keep it up indefinitely. Pow-puh-pow, pow-puh-pow-pow, pow. It would only be a matter of time before he couldn't stand it any longer. Humans are so predictable. Pow-puh-pow-puh . . .

I heard footsteps, then The Master opened the door. "*All right you stupid cat, come in.*"

Up I jumped once more. Best to placate him a bit and get back to my original intention of being the center of his universe. This time I reached out my paws to him in a kind of "won't-you-be-my-neighbor" supplication.

He hesitated.

11

Ah, one rule in alpha maleness, never let 'em see the crack in your veneer. And at that moment I got a glimpse into his soul. Why, maintaining the aura of alpha male might just be exhausting. And lonely. What with all that huffing and puffing that accompanies most alpha males, it's virtually impossible to show your soft side.

But I saw it and seized the moment. I crept into his arms and put my paws around his neck. He sighed and supported me with one arm while petting me with the other.

"Hey, come look at this crazy cat!"

The Mrs. arrived in an instant, no doubt eager to behold what fabulous new characteristic I had exhibited.

"Oh, isn't that cute? He's actually giving you a hug."

I don't much fancy the word "cute." I rather think the entire maneuver had been very clever. But I can't help myself with the hugging. I'm really quite affectionate as opposed to Miss Antisocial upstairs under the bed.

And in the end it turned out to be a huge win for me. For as I said before, I am certainly clever, and I had just managed to convince The Master I was, indeed, the new center of his universe.

Chapter Three

The Canines in My Life

Since Maggie the dog already lived here when I arrived, this posed a bit of a problem at first. I couldn't demonstrate my alpha maleness to her because she was a dog and totally oblivious to the fact that I am clearly the superior being. She was a small brown Chihuahua-terrier with one ear perpetually up and one ear down. I don't much like the large canines with their endless barking. Such a waste of energy that could be spent on something more worthwhile like a nap.

Which brings me to the need to detour from my narrative if you'll indulge me in a quick story about my superiority over the large canines across the street. They resided behind a tall fence that in and of itself must have caused the canines great frustration at not being able to see the goings on in the neighborhood happening right under their very noses. Each time they perceived a human walking down the sidewalk, mass hysteria ensued, as if they were missing out on possible prey. Another waste of time if one were to analyze the ultimate impossibility of chasing a human as canines seem wont to do. What could you conceivably hope for? The only possible reason for chasing prey is the ultimate goal of pouncing and killing swiftly.

I know what you're thinking and this is no time for squeamishness. I am a cat, and that is what we do. More about pouncing and killing later, but as a courtesy I'll warn you in advance in case you want to bury your head in the sand, pretend we aren't the mighty hunters nature intended us to be, and skip that chapter.

But on with my story. Whenever the opportunity presents itself to harass the opposite species, I am always up for the occasion. This particular technique of harassment I call the jump, sneer, and swish. After a quick furtive dash across the street, I pause in delicious anticipation.

They know I'm here.

I tense my legs, getting ready to spring. Wait. Watch for it. Just one more second before I finally leap to the top of the canines' fence in a display of impressive agility . . . and the crowd goes wild!

Then while thoroughly enjoying the ensuing pandemonium, and according to my mood, I either walk back and forth across the fence (another impressive talent of cats, we can easily balance on a fence rail, putting one foot perfectly in front of the other as we glide elegantly along), or I sit, whichever strikes my fancy, then I sneer at the brainless canines as they try to jump and lunge at the fence. Another wasted effort, as we both know a dog will never scale a high fence, and if he somehow manages to defy nature and land up there, he would topple off in an embarrassing show of splayed legs and paws attended by much yelping and whimpering that's sure to accompany said toppling. Ah, I'm forming a picture in my mind that's managing to cause me such exhilaration, I'm losing my focus.

I'LL TELL YOU WHAT I THINK

I sense you're hoping that it is at least a friendly sneer as we were neighbors and such, and it would have been considerate of me to give them more of a smile than a sneer. Au-contraire, no such luck. My sneer was positively dastardly. I always say if you're going to torment a canine, give it your all.

Let me just finish this small detour with the rest of my canine-harassing technique, that of the swish. The swish is definitely the best part as the morons are in such a frenzy, they can't decide what to do next. Which incidentally – from where I'm sitting atop the fence - is absolutely nothing, but they will still give every indication they are planning to commence some sort of blood-letting.

By the way, don't confuse swishing with lashing. If ever you see me lash my tail back and forth, you'll know I am angry. Swishing on the other hand indicates contentment. This little foray across the street to torture the canines never failed to provide endless enjoyment whenever I felt the urge. Jump, sneer, swish, and wild, frustrated frenzy. That's my idea of a satisfying afternoon.

Now, back to Maggie. She really was a dear little thing, and we got along quite famously. I suppose it was her total lack of self-esteem that made her kowtow to me, which explains why we got along so well. She spent her days worshipfully trotting after the Mrs., upstairs, downstairs, from room to room, to and fro. It never failed, wherever you found the Mrs., Maggie could be found at her heels. The Master would remark that he always knew when the Mrs. came down the stairs, because he could hear the familiar ka-thunk, ka-thunk of Maggie dutifully coming down the stairs after her.

I used to ask Maggie why she never let the Mrs. out of her sight. "I want her to love me," she replied in a worshipful but yet plaintive tone.

"But of course she loves you," I pointed out. "You've heard her declare for all the world to hear that she loves you best." I was still smarting from that insensitive comment that I didn't for one minute believe, but yet still quite a blow to my ego.

"Oh, I don't know," she said doubtfully. "I just wish I could know for sure."

I cocked the whiskers above one eye. "She indulges you beyond anything."

I pictured the ongoing battle between The Master and the Mrs. as she slyly tried to sneak food from her dinner plate to her dog at her feet.

"How many times have I told you, don't feed the dog from the table!" he bellowed.

"I'm not!"

I suppose the Mrs. thought it couldn't be proven as Maggie had snapped up the tasty morsel, leaving no evidence with which to convict her mistress. The entire episode seemed a wanton display of shamelessness if you ask me.

I liked to witness these dinnertime antics from my favorite observation point, that of being draped across the seat of an adjacent chair where I could conveniently be a part of the family dining hour and monitor Maggie at the same time.

I sided with The Master. How the Mrs. could sit there and blithely deny the errant food dropping was beyond me. And the scraps, they just kept on coming, followed by the grand finale, that of doing the dishes. As the Mrs. removed the dishes from the table, she tenderly placed them on the floor to allow the one she loved best to happily lick each and every plate before placing them in the dishwasher.

"You've got spaghetti sauce on your nose," I would often tell Maggie. She was not one for personal hygiene. I had to stay away from her after she had rolled in—well, let's just say it wasn't *my* excrement. I had been bred with the sensibility to bury mine instead of leaving it lying there on the lawn. We might as well have sent out invitations to the flies.

I never could understand why Maggie's kibble-sized, vacuous brain failed to make the connection between loving the scent of her own *eau de cologne* and the insufferable baths in the kitchen sink. The Mrs. only had to turn on the faucet when the shaking began, and I have to admit Maggie's performance was excellent.

"Look at you shaking like you're freezing to death. It's not going to work, you're still going to get a bath. You reek!" the Mrs. would scold.

At this point I felt hopeful there would be a blast of cold water attended by a harsh scrubbing to remove a patch or two of fur. Let the punishment fit the crime, I always say. But the Mrs. seemed blind to the necessity of taking the upper hand where Maggie's flagrant violation was concerned. No, in her moment of weakness, the Mrs. would ensure the water temperature to be just right. Why, there was no end to the spoiling.

"Just bathe her outside on the lawn!" The Master would complain.

"No, she'll get cold!"

"She's a dog!"

And with a nod of total disrespect to The Master's wishes, she snapped Maggie up and deposited her in the sink.

Although I must say the final scene turned out to be quite comical and amusing. After the Mrs. had lovingly removed the offending odor and toweled her off, she would place a dry towel on the floor and let Maggie go to work.

"Look, she's drying herself off!" she would gleefully exclaim.

If the grandkids happened to be visiting, they would all gather around and watch the impressive agility of someone who wasn't always operating on all four legs. Maggie would hurl herself to one side while pushing off with her hind legs in an almost running motion, sending her body rotating in a circle. Then she would flip over to the other side. Spin, dry, repeat. Next came the inevitable drying of the back, but any dog could accomplish this task. The drying of the neck and sides won my admiration.

And then when she had succeeded in doing her worst to the towel, she would run into the living room and finish drying on the carpet, repeating with both sides and her back. The closing act would then be a good rub to her hind end as she scooted her rump across the carpet. I was always careful to avoid that area, as I had inevitably just washed my paws and didn't want to soil them with whatever bit of feculence might have been remaining.

And then there was my cousin, Duke. Such an unpleasant excuse for a dog I have yet to meet. Yes, another Chihuahua in the family; these people simply had no imagination. Can you imagine naming a Chihuahua 'Duke,' as if he had somehow been mistaken for a Great Dane? The Master unapologetically calls him *Dookie*, and I must say, I wholeheartedly agree with this moniker for such a distasteful relative.

The day we first met will forever be indelibly etched upon my mind. I was lying at the top of the stairs surveying my domain and keeping an eye on the front door, my body sandwiched between two of the banisters with one paw outstretched for a quick swatting at whatever passed by if necessary, when in walked Duke with his mistress. I sprinted out of there and down the stairs in a flash, my senses on high alert against this rodent who had just entered the threshold of *my* kingdom. I gave a few angry hisses to set the tone.

He froze.

And I have to admit I did, too. We were both at a total loss for words as we tried to decide what to make of each other.

"Look at them, they are exactly the same," exclaimed the Young Miss, who obviously found the entire situation quite amusing. *"They're the same height, body size, and coloring. They're both black and white!"*

What? Both black and whites? He was no more black and white than I a tabby, but yet he was trying to pass himself off as one. I felt so insulted, if I'd had a spare hairball to huck up at that very moment, I most certainly would have. How dare he? The stunning beauty of my coloring compared to his: a counterfeit player painted totally black with just a schmear of white plastered haphazardly across his chest. I venture to surmise someone who'd had one too many saucers of milk had let loose with both the black paint and his self-control, only remembering to throw in a quick blast of white as a signature flourish at the last minute.

Where I had a gentle whisper of white lacing the surface of my nose, his was a boring solid black.

"And they both have white paws!"

White paws? I did a double take and narrowed my eyes to mere slits. Yes, you could possibly call them that, but mine were spectacular. His paws looked like the saucer imbiber had come to the end of the white spray and only managed to deliver a quick burst before calling it good. And the white of my chest began in a striking V and expanded up to embrace my neck like a collar, truly eye-catching in its splendor. No, he most certainly was *not* a black and white in the true sense. The Young Miss needed to have her eyes examined.

At that critical juncture I deemed only one action left to be taken. It had to be swift and all-encompassing so as not to leave even a hint of a doubt in Duke's mind as to whose house it was and who would forever be the alpha male.

I pounced on him like raccoons on cat food. As a nod to the ever-present hatred between cats and dogs, I went to work, and let me tell you I was in rare form.

"Reeeeeeeeeeer," I screamed, enlisting the aid of my claws in a brilliant parry and thrust maneuver. It must have been quite a sight to behold with the flurry of black and white fur flying every which way as Duke tried to extricate himself from my clutches.

"Yelp, yelp, yelp, yelp," he cried.

What a wimp. Was this the best he could do? No engaging on his part, no instinct to kill or be killed? I thought he'd have more fight in him than to immediately start waving the white flag about with his urgent yelping. I at least expected a ferocious growl.

I'LL TELL YOU WHAT I THINK

"Thor!" the Young Miss yelled.

I ignored her and continued to commence the work of death.

"Thor!" she yelled again.

I heard her the first time. Did she think I was deaf? I had no time for blind obedience in this life and death situation. I screeched even louder, threw him a right hook, and vowed I would fight to my dying breath.

I'm quite pleased at what I was able to accomplish before the Young Miss managed to separate us and caused me sudden embarrassment by grasping me firmly under the belly. If there's anything a cat hates, it's being scooped up like an old "scent"-soaked blanket being marched off to the rubbish bin. I immediately went limp as a dead mouse, for the Young Miss had quite an impressive grip, and resisting would only prove to be futile. I issued forth with a few good hisses instead.

That little act of defiance ended me up in solitary for the next few hours. Unfortunately, solitary happened to be the Young Miss's room where Juno resided under the bed. I glanced across the room and saw her eyes peering out from her cave of darkness.

"What are you looking at?" I demanded, although I knew any vocal exchange would be a waste of my valuable time. For we had never even exchanged two words, as she preferred the silent treatment in all of her interactions with yours truly.

Still smarting from the rather abrupt termination of my altercation with Duke, I began to prowl about the room. If I could at least engage in a good verbal sparring with the uncommunicative Juno, I might at least be able to assuage my wounded feelings. How could the Young Miss treat me like no more than a discarded piece of rubbish? Didn't she understand the absolute importance of establishing my dominance over Duke? This was an outrage, I tell you, an utter outrage! I continued to prowl and sulk while working out what to do with all of my pent-up frustration.

And then, as if by some stroke of good fortune, the solution handily presented itself. For there lying in the corner, I spied the Young Miss's favorite blanket, fairly beckoning to me, with one soft and furry corner tossed irresistibly askew in open invitation. With singular purpose, I marched over to that enticing blanket, positioned my posterior at the perfect angle, and released my bottled-up disgruntlement then and there. Ah, such a sweet feeling of revenge as I discharged my "scent" into that blanket.

I'll show you who's boss, I thought. Just try messing with the alpha male in this house and suffer the consequences. You think you can lock me in here, do you? Well, there's more than one way to skin a dog. (You didn't actually think I would be so vulgar as to say "skin a cat," did you? How revolting. On the other hand, skinning a dog is quite an appealing thought, for the world could always use one less of those annoying miscreants.)

Eventually I was released from solitary, but my misdeed committed while being held captive had been well worth it. Unfortunately, Duke ended up being a permanent part of the extended family, he being my cousin and all, but even with the short time I had been allowed to establish my dominance, Duke must have gotten my point, for he avoided me assiduously during his visits. Naturally, I was more than happy to drive home my message that I remained clearly in charge. A hiss on my part and a whimper on his (it became a game after a while) established the fact that I would forever be the alpha male, and he would remain the inferior (and feckless) dog.

Chapter Four

Resident Evil

I gave up trying to sleep on the Young Miss's bed with the always unfriendly Juno, so I moved into The Master and Mrs.' bedroom. Of course, The Master wasn't too happy about my choice, nor was Maggie who slept in one of our beds nearby. The Master and I played a game of on-off, on-off, but knowing he had to fall asleep at some point, I seized my chance and jumped up to find a nice, cozy spot for some needed slumber.

And on one of these nights I lay sprawled between The Master and the Mrs., quite enjoying the vast amount of real estate I had managed to secure right smack in the center of the bed, when the Mrs. suddenly sat up.

"Honey, wake up. Do you hear that?"

"What?" The Master mumbled, half awake.

"That scratching sound. Do you hear it?"

He lay still and listened. I heard it too, and it was definitely a scratching sound.

"It sounds like it's coming from the ceiling," she said.

"It is," he said, *"It's coming from the attic."*

"What is it?"

"I don't know."

"It sounds like birds or something. It gives me the creeps."

Birds? Now that's something I'd like to sink my teeth into. Give me the chance and I'll put an end to that scratching sound.

Over the next few nights, the sound continued. Sometimes just a faint scratching could be heard, but at other times quite the swinging fete seemed to be taking place attended by much thumping and scrambling about. Rather made me want to break into a nice samba if only I'd had a delicate feline to join me.

Some nights these lively soirees even ended with shrieking. A domestic quarrel of some sort perhaps? The poor Master and Mrs. were certainly not getting much sleep as evidenced by the way they stumbled around during the day with their bleary and bloodshot eyes.

Finally taking matters into his own hands, The Master hauled a ladder upstairs, into the closet, and climbed through the entrance to the attic. I sat at the foot of the ladder waiting for the verdict.

Maggie had wandered in, curious about the outcome herself.

"What do you think it is?" she asked.

"I don't know," I replied, "but it's certainly not birds. They're not creative enough to produce that kind of rambunctious cacophony."

To pass the time, I amused myself by poking about in between The Master's shirts and the Mrs.' clothes, thoroughly enjoying a good frolic with a tie dangling from a pink striped blouse.

"Why do you do that?" Maggie asked.

"Do what?"

"Go crazy with things like that? I've seen you grabbing wildly at that little red dot the Young Miss shines all over the floor. You act like it's a mouse. It's just *a dot*."

Time for a little enlightenment.

"Oh it's not just a dot," I explained. "It's the most wonderful of opportunities presenting itself, like an empty box or a half-opened drawer."

"Exactly. I can't understand why you like crawling into a box or a drawer or The Master's suitcase when it's lying open on the bed. You know he'll get mad and yell at you because his clothes will have cat hair on them."

"Ah, but that's where you and I differ. You see it as yelling, and I see it as raising his voice in excitement. I like to think he's secretly pleased I went out of my way to give his luggage such individualized attention. I keep telling you, you need to have more self-confidence."

I took a brief moment to think of an example. "Take that infernal barking of yours. You annoy the entire household letting us all know when so much as a leaf drops. And what does The Master always do?"

"He yells at me," she answered sullenly.

Actually, she was right. He *was* yelling at her, but I can't say I blame him. Why do dogs insult our intelligence by breaking into an ear-splitting notification that the doorbell has just rung?

I continued. "When they raise their voices as if they're mad, what's the worst that can happen? They'll carry on for a minute or two as humans do, and then they'll feel better because they actually believe they've managed to discipline us. But what do they actually *do*? Nothing. They love us to no end.

We're their beloved *pets*, which connotes rubbing our fur and talking to us the same way they talk to those small humans they wrap up in blankets and hold in their arms."

She sighed. "I suppose you're right, but that still doesn't explain why you're having fun trying to grab a tie that's not ever going to come off that blouse."

I paused for a moment to consider the best way to explain the concept of *joie de vivre* to someone as simple-minded as Maggie.

"Ah, I've got it. Why do you break into your happy dance when the Mrs. comes home?"

She seemed afraid to answer in case I was asking a trick question. "Because I'm happy she's finally home?" she asked cautiously. Poor thing, even when she talked to me, she was afraid of getting the answers wrong.

"Yes, you're happy! And at that very moment you can't help yourself, so you start jumping up and down in gleeful abandonment. Right?"

I could see a light enter her eyes, as if baby mice were beginning to run about her brain. "Yes, I guess I am happy," she agreed.

"That's what I'm trying to tell you. You have to stop and smell the catnip. You have to seize the moment when it presents itself!"

And with that I dove into a pile of shoes with their fascinating shoelaces. Oh, the hours I could spend batting those luscious goodies about.

I could hear The Master descending the ladder. I abandoned the shoelaces and stood at attention.

I'LL TELL YOU WHAT I THINK

"Did you find out what it is?" the Mrs. asked from the bedroom.

"Oh I found out all right," he replied in a disgusted voice. *"It's raccoons!"*

Raccoons! Those lazy, conniving thieves. Many a night I've found them on the back patio carting away my dinner. Filthy marauders. They think nothing of procuring provisions without working for them. I've toiled tirelessly to earn my morsels with my endless display of affection and beguiling ways.

"How did they get into the attic?" the Mrs. asked.

He began folding up the ladder. *"They climbed up the chimney and scratched at the mortar until they were able to loosen enough bricks to work their way in."*

"Did you see any of them up there?"

"Yeah, I saw one. I shined the flashlight right into his eyes, but then he turned around and stuck his head back into the hole in the chimney and just sat there with only his butt sticking out."

That must have been quite a sight, staring at the corpulent posterior of such a vexatious irritant. What an imbecile, trying to play possum as if he hadn't been spotted.

"What we need" The Master said, *"is a raccoon trap."*

That's the spirit, I cheered. The Master has the situation well in hand, and soon it will be good riddance to the undesirable vagrants.

⁕

THE NIGHT IS WARM WITH a hint of a gentle breeze. With my ears at high alert and whiskers tuned in like sonar, my nocturnal exploring has begun. As much as I love hogging

The Master's bed, in the summer I prefer to spend my nights outdoors scouting the neighborhood. The Master and Mrs. assume I sleep all day because that's what we cats do. I'll allow them the ignorance of their assumptions, but the truth is I come dragging in the house each summer morning thoroughly exhausted from the previous night's foray.

On this particular night something wonderful has drifted sumptuously along the breeze, teasing and taunting me to discover the source of such delectation. I jump into action, running across the lawn, agilely springing to the top of the back gate – seven feet high as I've heard The Master tell it – and bound across the front lawn to the flowering plum tree. Scaling a tree is my usual plan of attack when analyzing a perplexing situation. I am definitely getting closer, and the emanating whiff of *le poisson* is about to drive me mad. Higher, must climb higher.

With an effortless leap, I am onto the roof over the front porch, which leaves one more mountain to climb. And this mountain might as well be Mt. Everest, let me tell you, for I am on a mission, and failure is not an option. Springing one last time, I am onto the second story roof of the house.

Perhaps I should pause for a moment of silence as you consider my arresting athletic ability in arriving at this destination. When I stop to picture a human trying to climb a ladder while teetering and tottering in sheer terror, I guffaw at such sophomoric antics. Put yourself out of your misery, leave the experienced climbing to me, and return to the safety of terra firma.

I run across the wooden shakes of the roof toward the Promised Land where my gluttonous utopia awaits. Soon, my darling, my bewitching *bouillabaisse*. Soon we will be together, never to be parted.

And suddenly it is there, the ambrosial offering having been lovingly deposited in a small container and sitting in a little metal house. I am overcome with joy at finding the small abode that surely must have been custom-made explicitly for *moi*. For I love enclosed spaces; they are my Achilles' heel, and I am powerless to resist them. But no matter, for I am in paradise this night, and I will enter and imbibe to my heart's content.

I run inside to the fishy delight when suddenly the door slams shut. What is this??

I am trapped.

Betrayal, that's what I feel. How could The Master have gone to such lengths to lure me with this delicacy – and in a little metal house no less – and then lock me in?

I am despondent at the thought of spending the entire night here without so much as a cushion to curl up on, and as the hours pass, my protests become louder and louder. Get me out of here! I demand, but I have been completely, desolately ignored.

Long after the sun finally comes up the next morning, I hear The Master climbing a ladder to rescue me.

"Stupid cat! What are you doing up here? How did you manage to get yourself caught in a raccoon trap?"

Stupid cat? STUPID CAT? What an embarrassing *faux pas* on his part, to blame the cat for his debacle. He should have tried the door before presenting the little metal house to me with the love offering tenderly placed in a small container. I am *not* stupid, I am the cleverest of clever, the most splendidly amazing creature one could ever behold. I don't believe for one minute that was a raccoon trap. It was a little metal house made just for me with a door that needs to be adjusted.

⁂

THE NIGHT IS WARM WITH a slight breeze. A furry creature dashes quickly across the lawn, but I am not interested in a game of cat and mouse, for the enticing smell of something with wings has caught my attention. It entices, then tortures with a punishing aroma I am powerless to resist. I must find it, I must.

Back up the tree, onto the roof, and once again I see my little metal house. Inside a new receptacle has been deposited, and it is from whence the beguiling aroma emanates.

Well, The Master must have repaired the obnoxious door, else why the repeated taunting and teasing with the elixir of the gods that came from something with wings? Inside I crawl to sink my teeth into the soft and inviting delicacy. Bam!

No, I don't believe it! Surely The Master has a cruel sense of humor. He must be angry about the little pile of undigested food I left on the kitchen table. Can I help it if I have a delicate stomach that is easily prone to regurgitation? What was I to do, bat the assemblage of my evacuated stomach content across the table and deposit it in his chair? At least I left it where he could easily spot it instead of dumping it in a pile for the unsuspecting arrival of his *derrière*.

Well, this time I won't be left out here all night. I feel like I'm sitting in a cage at the pound waiting for someone to adopt me. I start with a long, mournful wail. I feel the double betrayal from the bottom of my heart, incensed at The Master's idea of a joke. Why I might just retaliate by leaving a little of my "scent" in the corner of his new man cave, nicely hidden behind the easy chair. I can see it now running down the edges of the gleaming white floorboard in delicate yellow rivulets.

"Let me out!" I shout. "How could you do this to me twice? I thought you loved me!"

Suddenly a light is shining in my eyes, and I hear The Master's voice coming from the open window.

"You are the dumbest cat I have ever seen. Not once, but twice getting yourself stuck in the raccoon trap."

I cannot believe The Master is still blaming me for his ineptitude. Yes, go ahead and make me the scapegoat. I picture him tinkering about with the door for a minute or two and then simply placing it on the roof and hoping for the best. And to think I seriously had high hopes in his ability to rectify the situation.

Amateurs.

I let fly an especially angry complaint at the shameful inequity of the situation.

And then displaying a most discreditable behavior, The Master actually had the audacity to laugh. *"If you're stupid enough to get yourself trapped twice, you can just stay there until morning."*

I know that tone of voice, and it would appear my goose is cooked.

But wait, there might be hope, for the Mrs. has entered the scene.

"How did he get in there?" she asked.

"I put a can of cat food in the trap. He's about the same size as a raccoon, so when he ran in to eat the cat food - as the raccoons were supposed to do - the trap door shut behind him."

Oh yes, go ahead and try to cover up your ineptitude. That little metal house is not a raccoon trap, it's a gift presented to me by The Master who now is blaming me for his poor skills as a handyman. This entire situation has been caused by you not fixing the broken door!

"But you can't leave him there all night!" the Mrs. pleaded.

"Of course I can. I'm not climbing up on the roof in the dark."

She remained silent, which I did not view as an encouraging sign. Come on, I urged with another wail, you can talk him into it. Surely you don't want to leave a poor, helpless kitty (I use this term when I'm playing the sympathy card) up here on the roof, so far up I could fall and get hurt.

The truth is, when cats fall, they almost always land on their feet. I will reflexively course correct as I'm falling, under the direction of my eyes and ears, shifting my balance to land adroitly on my feet.

Every time.

But I am certain she won't stop to think about this often-overlooked fact, because she has a tender heart and her common sense will be overridden by concern for my well-being. And so I continue to plead my case.

"Do you think he'll be okay?"

Oh no, I know the path this conversation is taking, and I'm quite certain I've lost the battle. She has let her compassion for her beloved cat be trumped by The Master's refusal to rescue me in the middle of the night. And in his ridiculously funny nightclothes, I might add.

Fine, two can play at this game. If you ever try to entice me with cuisine from something with wings placed inside a little metal house, I shall rebuff your every effort.

I'LL TELL YOU WHAT I THINK

And that's all I have to say about my two insultingly uncomfortable nights inside the little metal house with the broken door.

Chapter Five

Entertaining

Life with The Master and the Mrs. is one endless party with a never-ending array of guests coming and going. There are the usual suspects, the Young Miss's two siblings who arrive bearing miniature humans (aka "the grandkids") anxious to throw small objects about from room to room and clamoring for unhealthy vittles. I usually observe the pandemonium from the safety of The Master's shoulder, taking note of sticky puddles I will want to avoid after they and their attendant bedlam have finally departed.

And then there are the various and sundry freeloaders happily settling in for an evening of sumptuously prepared fare and lively conversation. Unfortunately Duke often arrives uninvited, anxious to spend the evening obnoxiously begging the Mrs. for kibbles and affection.

These evenings are spent in my backyard where the occupants gather around a large table and gorge themselves. Then after removing several layers of body wear, they all jump into the swimming pool with much yelling and splashing about.

The story is told of the young miss's previous cat Kitty - previously named Princess, then changed to Darla (this name truly makes me pause), then finally just called Kitty - standing behind the Mrs., who scooted her chair back rather abruptly, startling the poor thing so severely that she jumped into the air and landed on something used in the pool called a noodle. It was apparently rather comical as Kitty used some fancy footwork, desperately shuffling her feet in a running fashion as the noodle rotated round and round, eventually landing her in the water. It must have been quite a sight, as cats do not swim.

The Mrs. was hollering *"Poor Kitty!"* while trying to extricate the drowned rat by reaching in with her bare hands for the rescue. Not a wise choice, as Kitty latched on with her extremely sharp, serrated molars, hanging on for dear life. Let me just ask you: Have you ever really observed these magnificent specimens inside a cat's mouth? You may want to skim past this part if you're squeamish, but let me just tell you we use these sharp, serrated molars to remove muscle and connective tissue away from the bone of a small animal and create bite-sized pieces to be swallowed whole.

No complaints about this previous explanation, please. This is how I was created. Humans can be quite hypocritical when it comes to their disapproval of my eating habits, because I've seen the overindulgence that takes place at The Master and Mrs.' dinner parties. And upon observation of such gluttony, sometimes I feel a little nauseated myself. Now Duke and Maggie on the other hand, well, I'll get to that in a minute. But back to the harrowing near-drowning of Kitty.

After removing her from the pool and forcing the vicelike jaws apart to remove Kitty's teeth from the Mrs.' hand, the episode was soon forgotten until the next morning when she woke up to find her hand twice the size it had been the previous day.

This involved an immediate visit to the doctor for a shot of some sort or other, and I can truly sympathize. The Master takes me to the doctor for my shots on a too-frequent basis, and I can tell you it's an awful place that smells like fear, canine urine, and death. So my heart went out to the Mrs. in the retelling of this story. Now Kitty, on the other hand, I wouldn't waste any tender feelings for her. She was apparently dim-witted to begin with and should have had the brains to avoid getting that close to the water.

The pool in my backyard had a blue cover that, when closed, had the appearance of looking like a pond from the air. Even more so when it had rained a few inches and it truly looked like a nice, deep pond. Which was a great temptation for the local ducks of the area. They would circle above, planning the curve of their trajectory just so, and make a beeline for the assumed pond for a nice swim. I have never come so close to a guffaw when I witnessed them hitting the cover and, in meeting the resistance of a solid surface, tumbled head over webbed feet. I say *close* to a guffaw, because I have far too much class to ever break out into a guffaw. But an entertaining sight it was, nonetheless.

I could see their pebble-sized brains working furiously as they tried to figure out what on earth had just happened. The dazed – and no doubt slightly bruised – ducks would then crawl off of the cover to sit on the side and recuperate. Oftentimes it had rained several inches, and they would gingerly climb back on the cover, giving it a second go around until they got the hang of the shallowness and began carefully gliding about.

These uninvited fowl were such frequent visitors - especially during mating season – that the Young Miss named them George and Isabel, and thus they were called by one and all despite the ever-changing courting couples. Personally, they all look alike to me. The Georges were all brown with green heads, and the Isabels were entirely brown, a rather boring species if you ask me.

And uninvited they were, for their ill-mannered inappropriate elimination left wet, white, inky-type puddles all around the pool. Inasmuch as I lick my paws on a frequent basis, I was ever vigilant in carefully watching where I stepped. I won't offend you by describing what their Montezuma's revenge tasted like, but suffice it to say I *have* tasted it, and it is horrible. The Master, upon discovering this inappropriate elimination, would holler in disgust as he was inevitably the one left to clean up after them. For some reason the Mrs. always seemed to be absent when this chore needed to be done.

During one of these sprightly evenings after the participants had consumed enough food to feed a small country, George and Isabel decided to fly in and join the party. The winged couple waddled back to rest under a tree, conversing with each other in low voices.

Maggie had just gulped down an entire hot dog whole, while I wandered over to the sidelines to observe what would inevitably come next.

As I had anticipated, Maggie only managed a few steps before her body began to be wracked with convulsions. She froze and stiffened her body in an unnatural fashion, arching her back and erupting into a detonation of hacking and yakking until the hot dog had been regurgitated back out in its entirety.

The reverberations must have startled George and Isabel, because they issued forth in startled, resonant quacks, rapidly flapped their wings in fervor, and flew up to land on the roof of the patio.

"Watch this," The Master said to the tableful of onlookers.

This should be good, I thought, incorrectly assuming he was going to teach Maggie a lesson. The Master seemed to enjoy these little episodes of teaching and correction to no end, as the varied and different methods were really quite impressive. He even had a different name for each of what he called his "teases."

I very quickly found that The Master had not been referring to Maggie the Gormandizer, but to George and Isabel's erstwhile flight to the roof. For there I sat minding my own business: neither classlessly begging for food like Duke, nor expelling it soon after like Maggie, but simply lounging lazily on the sun-warm bricks surrounding the pool (a sufficient distance away from the guests so as not to repeat Kitty's unfortunate pool dunking episode) when The Master abruptly stood up, strode over to where I lay reclining, scooped me up like a bag of dog food, and launched me into the air.

And for a few uncontrollably frightening moments, I found myself flying through the air at full velocity, with the sudden dawning realization that the intended target was George and Isabel. With very little time to course-correct my body so as to land on my feet, I unceremoniously dropped from the sky and landed in the middle of the unsuspecting couple.

I can only imagine the terror experienced on the part of George and Isabel at the sudden flight and appearance of Super Cat (minus the black mask and cape), for they began squawking and shrieking and immediately resumed their act of inappropriate elimination in short, quick bursts as I danced about in polka fashion to dodge the rapid-fire, torpedo like expulsions. My cries were as much a fear of sullying my paws as being in such close proximity to these winged fowl that suddenly seemed about to take a giant chomp out of my midsection with their hammer-like bills. In the ensuing milieu, I felt hard pressed to decipher where their cacophonous quacking ended and my hissing and screeching began.

I maintain that I am a mighty warrior with an as-yet undefeated title when it comes to hunting and killing robins or sparrows, but there is a monumental difference in size between these small, easy prey and George and Isabel.

And my options, as I viewed them, were not all that appealing. For whereas I had only feigned flight, these two could actually accomplish this task quite effortlessly. Were I to leap from the patio roof onto the roof of the house in an attempt to escape, they could have simply engaged their natural aeronautics in hot pursuit.

And were I to attempt to drop all the way to the ground, I could possibly land on my feet as I had – every time – up to this point in my quickly-coming-to-an-end life. But this was a height I had never before attempted to jump from, creating a sudden, unpleasant vision of Thor fricassee served up with a side of entrails and a dash of parsley.

And so with these unappealing options, I chose simply to act the part of Super Cat (minus the black mask and cape) arching my back, screaming like someone had stepped on my tail, and continuing to scare the feathers right off George and Isabel. An absolute multiplicity of feathers were flying all over the place along with whatever else they had been expelling, scattered helter-skelter from one side of the roof to the other.

And I can assure you that mess could not be cleaned with even a week of heavy rain. No, The Master would have to get up there and scrub it himself. Which would serve him right after what he did to me. Personally, I hoped it involved some slipping and sliding on his part, as he would inevitably be forced to dodge the oozing puddles produced by the dazed and frightened couple.

He eventually did arrive to rescue me. After much pleading on the part of the Mrs. he retrieved a ladder and climbed up to the roof, laughing the entire time.

This had been a horrific experience, but let me take this moment to demonstrate how I handled it with grace and class. For the lesson to be learned from this dismaying episode is how you behave once the rude and inconsiderate act has finally come to an end. After being deposited on terra firma, I affected an impressive air of nonchalance, paused to give a few good licks to my nether regions with legs splayed for the benefit of the party guests and in an offensive salute to The Master, then sauntered away.

Minus the black mask and cape.

Chapter Six

Libations and Forbidden Fare

The Mrs. could be quite uptight about keeping a tidy house. If The Master left the dinner table to retrieve the salt, she made short work of his dishes.

"What did you do with my plate? I wasn't finished eating!"

"Oh," she said efficiently, *"I thought you were done."*

She retrieved a washrag and vigorously scrubbed an invisible spot on the counter. The Mrs. had absolutely unrealistic expectations in case company should arrive unannounced and someone – heaven forbid – might judge her to be a sloppy housekeeper.

"It's our house," The Master would argue, *"It looks lived in!"*

"Well, I like it to look like a magazine ad! No one wants to visit someone who has a dirty house!"

I harbored secret hopes he would get the upper hand in this ongoing battle, but she would have none of it. She did, however, compromise to the extent of letting him leave his drinking glass on the table in case he wanted to revisit it later. (She kept her glass on the table as well which puzzles me no end, because I would think her cleanliness fetish dictated the amount of time she would allow her glass to remain soiled before washing and returning it to the shelf.)

Personally, I feel entitled to drink from the family's glasses left on the table, affording me a welcome opportunity to partake as I see fit. Else why leave them on the table where I can easily jump up and have a drink? What a thrill to hop up on the table and imbibe a cup of nice fresh water and, if there's more than one, I must try them all!

Which brings me to one of my absolutes in life. *Never* drink out of a container sitting on the floor. For one, I am not about to share Maggie's water dish which is located right next to her bowl of kibbles. How can I be expected to drink a sip of water while being assaulted with the overpowering and slightly nauseating smell of dog food? And as for Juno? Let me paint a picture of walking by the bathroom and seeing Juno's back end sticking out from the toilet. Yes, that is where she finds liquid refreshment when she is thirsty.

And so with these two very unfavorable choices when it comes to enjoying a drink of water, I have decided I am certainly not going to drink out of these communal bowls like some sort of common alley cat. No, I have been bred for finer things, such as drinking out of a container that has only touched a human's lips.

And may I mention the very act of *how* a dog drinks? The loud *schlep, schlep, schlep* sound of their tongue hitting the water (which always makes me rather queasy) and knocking it carelessly into their mouths, is a good lesson on how not to drink. We felines drink daintily and politely with a soft *pew, pew, pew* sound, which is the correct way to drink I might point out. But as I said, I will never drink from a bowl sitting on the floor. And I will never, *never,* (I'm shuddering here at the mere thought) drink out of a toilet.

I'LL TELL YOU WHAT I THINK

If the humans had left the table, then the leftover glasses were simply too tempting to be ignored. There they sat, almost taunting me like some sort of prize to be won. Thus, I must accept the gauntlet they had offered and sample each one.

The Master got wise and took to drinking from a large red mug with a handle, a lid, and a large crack down the side. Finances must have been tight with all the soirees they threw and the copious amounts of food being consumed by the freeloaders. The cracked mug was a rather crass look for The Master if you ask me. He looked like a sailor tossing back a stein of beer after a long day of doing whatever sailors do. I rather expected some sort of "yo-ho" song to accompany his crass container-imbibing.

The Mrs. would often place a piece of paper over her water glass to keep me out, but her diligence waned at times, which led me to believe she secretly hoped I would help myself. And if she happened to slip and leave one uncovered, I would sample hers lovingly.

The Master's drinking glass - if I happened to find an open container instead of his cracked red mug - I sampled, but not lovingly. I was merely evening out the score since the Super Cat episode. Whenever he would see me enjoying a cool refreshment on the table or strolling along the kitchen counters, he would slap his hands loudly and utter forth with much hissing as if he were a cat. Again, not a good look for The Master.

And so I would pretend to obey him by dutifully scurrying off the table. Ah, it makes me chuckle inwardly when I think of how I had bamboozled him into thinking I was an obedient cat. I simply took to drinking with a sharp ear for the approach of his footsteps, to which I hopped down off the table until he left the room. Then I resumed my libations.

I will, however, confess to you privately that there is an art to judging the width of the opening when sticking one's head into the glass. It is with much embarrassment I concede to you I have gotten my head stuck as The Master and Mrs. stood laughing at my expense.

"He looks hilarious with his eyes stretched open and his ears plastered flat!" she remarked. No, I never repeated that exercise again.

I hate to give any more space on the page than is necessary to mention Duke, but I was quite happy to hear he was in the dog house - as it were - for a stunt he had pulled at dinner time. It seems his owners were trying out a new dog food that contained some suspicious green pellets being foisted off as "vegetables." (*Perish the thought.*)

I can picture with such gleefulness the surprise he must have experienced when he took his first mouthful. In one corner of his mouth were his favorite nuggets of "meat," (so they call it) and in the other, a new sickening attempt at "nutrition." I only wish I could have been there to watch the spectacle as he attempted to retain the "meat" while at the same time expelling the nutritious green pellets. Finally in desperation it seems he rushed over to the heater vent and deposited the counterfeit "vegetables" where he suspected no one would find them. What a moron. He obviously had never paid attention to what happens when a furnace comes on and through what device the heat actually flows. Take it from someone who spends much of his day lounging in front of the furnace vent. It would have taken no time at all to produce the stench that in turn landed him in the dog house.

But enough energy wasted on Duke. Back to my eating habits. Interestingly enough, I preferred cat food to human leftovers. I suppose it was the word *leftover* that seemed a true indication of what it truly professed to be, the half-eaten remains of something that had been alive a short time ago and that the humans no longer wanted, offered to the pets as if we were no more than an afterthought. No, I preferred my bowl of the cat food of my choosing, freshly poured and wafting with the delicate aroma of something with fins or wings.

Maggie, on the other hand, had no qualms about scarfing up anything and everything *left over*.

"Control yourself, Maggie," I would lecture, "Don't you have any sense of pride? You don't have to eat every discarded morsel in sight."

"Why?" she would ask vacuously.

"Well, for one thing, let me remind you of the hot dog eating incident that incited a riot on the part of George and Isabel." (Notice how I smoothly blamed the entire incident on her and her gluttonous eating.)

"You know those leftovers aren't going anywhere. Haven't you ever noticed how the Mrs. puts aside a hefty-sized pile for you to enjoy later?"

"I can't help myself," she admitted. I did admire her candid honesty, even though she was unwilling to heed my advice.

"*Why* can't you help yourself?" I prodded, knowing full well the answer.

"I'm afraid I'll never get any more leftovers."

"But that's absolutely absurd. Do you think The Master and Mrs. will suddenly stop eating?"

She furrowed her brows. "Well, no, but . . ."

"But what?"

The Master had just issued forth a *"Don't feed the dog from the table!"* when Maggie paused to catch a piece of meat midair. I have to give her credit, for no matter the size of her brain, she had amazing coordination when it came to catching food thrown her way. I can only imagine what a fine bird catcher Maggie would make under my excellent tutelage. She was a dead-on accurate catch, a sight to behold really, earning my much sought-after admiration. Which I can assure you is not easily won as I tend to dole it out in small portions only when I am feeling charitable.

Duke, on the other hand, was so feckless, the most he could attempt was an ill-timed scurry for the morsel after it had landed squarely on his nose and bounced onto the floor.

"But what?" I repeated to Maggie. "What do you think will happen if you exercise a little self-restraint and actually eat less?"

She stared at me uncomprehendingly. "Why would I want to eat less? People food tastes so good, I want as much of it as I can get."

I felt the large gulf that existed between us. Dogs are absolute gluttons that don't know when to quit, and Maggie was no exception. I could see I would be wasting my time trying to introduce her to the refined concept of small nibbles apportioned throughout the day, delicately eaten in leisure moments of quiet contemplation.

Nor do I blame her really. Who knows what disgusting oddities dog food is made of? My food is at least made of something with wings or something that swims. No wonder she waits to eat her contemptible dog food only after the dinner dishes have been finished and the Mrs. has turned off the light and left the kitchen.

And when she would finally make her way to her bowl, Maggie had two interesting eating habits: She would gather a mouthful of pellets, walk a few steps away, drop them all out onto the floor, and then proceed to eat each morsel one at a time.

I once inquired why she engaged in this strange inclination.

"I'm pretending they're little pieces of people food the Mrs. has left for me."

Someone else might give this explanation no additional thought, but upon further cogitation I have gleaned this unique way of eating is simply an outward expression of her continued insecurities.

I did not, however, reveal this observation to her, for it was a concept her little brain would be incapable of grasping. (The ostentatious – and yes, even vulgar – demonstration of the Mrs.' undying love for her little companion could only be misconceived by someone with a diminutive brain.) Which of course explains Maggie's failure to understand to what excess the Mrs. loved her.

I suppose it was ingrained in her species, really. Name me any dog who doesn't fawn over his master's every move, and I'll cry foul. No, the art of playing hard to get is beyond a canine's comprehension, for he is too moronic to understand the concept.

And Maggie's second habit of eating I have deduced as simply an idiosyncrasy deficient of further psychological meaning. She would consume the food on one entire side of the bowl and leave the other side full, creating a sort of visually artistic Andy Worhol-type linear slant design in her dog food bowl. I imagine if some misdirected humans were to study this ingenious creation long enough, they would have declared it a sign from God as they glimpsed the Virgin Mary in repose.

Indeed the brown pellets were piled so artfully, this exercise must have required all of Maggie's skillful agility to create such a masterpiece, and which explains why I did not wholly categorize Maggie as falling entirely into the moronic canine category.

And as long as we're on the subject of Maggie's diet, she actually preferred cat food. But The Master and Mrs. forbid it. Hence they placed my cuisine up high where only I could get to it. She also preferred kitty-box crunchies too, which entailed sneaking into the litter box and happily snacking away on my or Juno's tootsie rolls. No wonder she had such vile breath.

Nor did I understand her revolting habit of dropping several nuggets onto the carpet and then walking away, leaving them untouched. (My deepest sympathies went out to the Young Miss who occupied the room where this brazen behavior took place.) As I ruminated upon Maggie's possible reasoning for depositing and then abandoning her stolen waste upon the floor, I could only surmise she was anxious to save some mouth-watering treats for later.

I'LL TELL YOU WHAT I THINK

The Master actually had the audacity to blame *me* for Maggie's contemptible behavior. Can you imagine me not leaving my own feces in my commode? The entire exercise of my elimination is a shameful enough act requiring total privacy and accompanying much embarrassment and furtive glancing about. And then for good measure – or overkill if you insist – to remove all evidence of the embarrassing act that has occurred, I bury it.

After going the extra mile to ensure no trace is left, why would I then uncover it and drag it out to the carpet? And let me add that I am absolutely dripping with *je ne sais quoi,* which forbids me from doing something as repulsive as that to which I was being accused.

But enough about Maggie and her puzzling and revolting eating habits. Back to me, the central focus of this story, and drinking choices.

Drinking from a glass is wonderful, but as there have been times when I've had to delicately extricate my face because I may have miscalculated the width of the glass, therefore I have been able to convince the females in the house to refresh me directly from the faucet. It's amazing how gullible they are, really. I suppose I *could* drink from a common container on the floor if push came to shove, but why stoop so low when I could just as easily train these women to do my bidding?

Pay attention to how it's done. You jump up on the bathroom counter when they are in the middle of their *toilette* and wait for the water to begin streaming from the faucet. This might require some fortitude as they try to bat you away, but downright pushiness will win out every time. Your best shot will be when they start brushing their teeth (a human behavior that I for one do not comprehend). They invariably will have to turn the water on, and there's your chance. Get in there, man, and use your best bob-and-weave skills to achieve your intended goal. Be at the ready as soon as the toothbrush is waved through the stream of running water, because it will inevitably have to return to her mouth, leaving the water running for your pleasure.

That's the moment you stick your head down and drink the ambrosia. Be quick about it, for the brush will be waved through the water again, but it will return once more to the mouth allowing you the opportunity to duck your head and resume your imbibing.

Up, down, up, down. Quite an enjoyable game actually. Just stick with it and you will remain the victor when she finishes with the toothbrush. Then you will be free from further impediment and may drink to your heart's content.

And don't be rushed. You have worked hard with your bobbing and weaving and have earned this opportunity. Ah, yes, she will stand there with her hands on her hips waiting for you to finish. She might even tap her feet impatiently and give a loud sigh in frustration while you drink deeply and leisurely. Just keep at it and she'll eventually give up and attend to some other obligation.

Then and only then do you stop drinking. For to do so in her presence will demonstrate weakness, and when you give a human a small opening, they heave it open and let all the cold air in. No, you are to remain in control of the situation and *always* retain the upper hand. For you are the alpha male.

I'LL TELL YOU WHAT I THINK

After I have consumed enough to water a camel, I jump down, lick my paws, and leap sprightly over to the bed for a nap.

❦

"OH MY GOODNESS, I FORGOT about the water. I wonder how long I've left it running!"

Chapter Seven

Brilliant Advice

The Mrs. bought me a wonderful gift of two beds to choose from. Maggie appeared to be under the impression one had been intended for her and one for me, but since I embraced the opportunity to sleep in either one whenever I pleased, I considered them both mine.

I would stand in front of the two inviting sleeping berths and wait for the mood to dictate which one would I would choose for my afternoon respite. Invariably as soon as I had drifted off into inviting slumber, Maggie would arrive and stand in front of my sleeping quarters.

"Why are you sleeping in my bed?" she would ask mournfully.

"What do you mean *your* bed?

"Well, you slept in the other bed yesterday, so I slept in this one."

"And?"

I felt slightly bad because I was taunting her, but only slightly, and certainly not enough to actually move from this luxurious, curled up position. I wrapped my tail around my legs and put one paw over my eyes, hoping she would take the hint.

"So why should I have to get your castoff every day?"

Castoff? Touché Maggie. I would give a point to you for your assertiveness, but unfortunately, you're not intelligent enough to know that's what you have actually demonstrated.

"Because I got here first," I said. "Do I come up to you when you're napping and demand you vacate?"

"No, but I don't come up here to nap, because I have to follow the Mrs. around the house. I only come here when she's not home."

True enough, and another point for Maggie. If we were keeping score. But we're not.

Fortunately, I always know how to win this argument, and that is simply by ignoring her, closing my eyes, and drifting off to sleep. Frequently I would throw in a little snore for good measure.

After some minutes of feeling her still hovering over my bed like a pesky mosquito, she would sigh and get into the other bed.

Now when she was on the bed with the Mrs., that was another matter. Forget assertiveness, she would behave more like a wolf. It was such an enjoyable game for me, I just couldn't resist seeing her fully engaged in protecting her territory and her mistress.

First, I would start by sauntering into the bedroom, which would cause Maggie's ear to fly straight up. A few more steps and she would sit up and stiffen every muscle in her body as if seized by rigor mortis. Now the real fun would begin.

Up I would hop, waiting for her to fly into action. Teeth bared, hackles up, she would come after me after as if defending the Mrs. from invading marauders.

"Maggie! Stop that!" she would yell at her little companion.

I'LL TELL YOU WHAT I THINK

Because I enjoyed the sport and to give Maggie the impression she had won round one, I would jump off and circle around to the other side for round two.

Up I jumped. Once again, teeth bared, hackles raised, chasing me off the bed.

"Maggie! Stop that!"

This was so entertaining, sometimes I would give it a go four or five good times until the Mrs. was at her wits' end, and she threw Maggie off for a cool-down period. Fine with me, I could wait. This was just too much fun.

After a few minutes of banishment – a shamefully short period if you ask me (the Mrs. is a weak disciplinarian when it comes to the one she "loves best") –Maggie hopped up on the bed and resumed her guarding of the Mrs.

I stretched out my front legs and flexed my paws. Time to spring into action. With Maggie absolutely in full guard mode, her eyes full of—what was it? Anger? Jealousy? Frustration that we both knew how this game would end? All of the above? I strutted in a deliciously deliberate, painstakingly, slow fashion to the top of the bed and sprang up to . . . the nightstand. One of my favorite pastimes is sitting directly under the lamp while I sun myself.

Oh the ire, the wrath of this gullible canine. In her rush to thwart my next move, charging blindly toward me and discovering too late that I had changed course and landed on the nightstand instead of the expected bed, it left her with nowhere else to go but into midair. Still perched under the lamp, I affixed an excellent poker face and watched her sail past only to land on the floor in an ungraceful splay of head and legs.

And to add insult to her poor injury, the Mrs. – I can only say in a moment of uncontrollable weakness – had the audacity to laugh. And this wasn't a chuckle or small, timid giggle. Nay, this was a loud, full-bellied laugh; that which comes from deep within when the scene to behold is the rare combination of absolutely perfect symmetry and brilliant choreography, resulting in no-holds-barred, unchecked delight.

"That will teach you to mess with Thor!"

Oh hey now, that's a rather insensitive (although true) remark. I must admit, at the Mrs.' lack of consideration for her loyal companion, I rather felt sorry for Maggie at the indignity she suffered with her mistress looking on. Expecting at least a modicum of understanding and sympathy from the one person who "loved her best," she instead had been met with a shocking and quite unladylike howl instead.

The idea had been for me to demonstrate my cunning ability to outsmart a dog through my own cleverness. I didn't need any help from the Mrs., for I am the master of my own universe and can deftly maneuver through every situation with finesse and agility. That and the fact that Maggie has a rather undersized brain.

As I watched Maggie walk dejectedly away and, feeling that the Mrs. had stolen my thunder, I removed myself from the lamp's warm glow and joined her. I turned around and gave the Mrs. a how-could-you double-entendre look. How could you have chortled at the one you "loved best," and how could you have stolen my thunder?

She must have read my mind (she does that sometimes) for she called out, *"Maggie, come back. I'm sorry."*

I'LL TELL YOU WHAT I THINK

I've heard the Mrs. called a gentle soul, and I quite agree. She would be heartbroken to know she had hurt Maggie's feelings.

Maggie plopped down on the rug in the hall and sighed. I wandered out and joined her, pausing to lick a spot on the back of my leg. I rolled an unnatural 180 degrees, a feat known only to cats who have incredibly flexible spines, and started on the underside of my belly. I happened to glance over at her with her head on her paws and noted the sad droop of her eyes.

I unfolded and sat up. "Maggie, the trouble with you is you need to stop being the victim."

She looked at me as if I were speaking in a different language, like aardvark. Hmm, this was going to be a bit of a challenge. It's a good thing I tolerated her well enough, for I could feel a nap coming on, and this might take a few minutes of my precious time.

I cogitated for a moment. How to break it down so a simpleton could understand. She had no idea how valuable this little teaching moment was. I didn't expend myself for just anyone; she should feel supremely complimented at the bestowal of my advice.

I started again. "Why do you try to attack me when I come near the Mrs.?"

She thought for a moment. "Because I'm jealous?"

"I'm sorry, was that a question?"

"What?"

"I think your answer was 'because I'm jealous' with a period at the end, not a question mark. Don't you know the reason?"

"I guess so."

61

"And what is the reason?"

"Probably because I'm afraid the Mrs. will love you best."

"But that's absurd. Not only is she dripping with affection and fawning over your every move, she says it frequently." (I'm still smarting from that reminder.)

"But she laughed at me!"

"Well, of course she did. It was hilarious. It's not every day you see a dog miss her intended target and go sailing through the air."

At that she gave a bit of a smile. Ah, that's the stuff. Now we're getting somewhere.

"You know when Duke's master grabs him and throws him into the pool? I saw you laugh the last time it happened."

She contorted her body into an unnatural position and began nipping at a flea.

"So tell me why you laughed," I said. "I'm sure Duke didn't appreciate it."

She stopped nipping and said, "But it was funny."

"Exactly."

"But it's not so funny when it's happening to me."

"Maggie, I'm going to give you some advice that will change your life."

She raised her eyebrows. She was all ears now. Or ear. As I mentioned before, one ear always stood straight up, so I assume she was now paying attention with the other one as well.

"The secret to having everyone love you all the time is being able to laugh at yourself."

She furrowed her brows. "Why would I want to do that?"

I'LL TELL YOU WHAT I THINK

"Because it will make you stop feeling sorry for yourself! You waste far too much time worrying about being loved. You need to stop that and tell yourself *everybody* loves me!"

"Well, yeah, everybody does love *you*."

I gave an impatient sigh. "No, Maggie, not me. *You*. From now on, you tell yourself that everybody loves *you*."

I watched her process this last bit and thought with any luck the dense, uncomprehending fog might have cleared in her tiny brain. For a modicum of time at least. I only hoped she could absorb this valuable piece of advice. And take note, dear reader, it's the best piece of advice you'll ever receive from a cat. Or anyone else for that matter.

"Do you really think it's true?" she asked doubtfully.

"Of course it's true. Why does the Mrs. let you do the dishes before they go into the dishwasher? And risk the wrath of The Master as she slyly sneaks a tender morsel to you under the table?"

"I guess you're right."

Brilliant! (On my part, not hers.) Now time for homework. "Okay, Maggie, I'm going to give you an assignment."

"A what?"

"I want you to do something."

"Okay."

"When we head outside with the family and their never-ending group of friends, when you think the Mrs. isn't paying you enough attention or you think no one loves you, or better yet, if you think people are laughing at you, I want you to burst out laughing at yourself and go run around the yard for joy."

Her face contained an expression of befuddlement.

"Just do it, Maggie, don't try to understand why. Will you do that? I promise it will make you a happier dog."

She sat silent for a moment, furrowing her eyebrows, and I pictured her mentally trying to line up all the dog bones in a row.

"What do you say? Will you do it?" I asked in my most impressive pep-talk voice.

"Oh, okay, I guess I can try it."

Chapter Eight

Sneak Attack

The evening is calm with a slight breeze. I must say, summer in my backyard is spectacular. Flowers are blooming in brilliant colors, bees from The Master's hives industriously fly from one blossom to another in a flurry of activity, and I am sprawled lazily on the warm bricks surrounding the pool. It's good to be king.

For I can't imagine expending such energy as a bee, laboring furiously in strict colony order, being given a brainless role to carry out for the betterment of the entire gang. A word I loathe? Cohesive. As in united, i.e., working together in hey-that's-the-spirit-let's-all-pull-together mode. Have you ever stood at the foot of a hive and watched two bees drag a poor dead fellow out the front door and launch him through the air to land on the ground?

A caution for those of you with tender sensibilities or small beings who might be reading this. Yes, I am speaking of death. These irritating humorless laborers go about this task without even pausing to say a few words about how brilliant the stripes on the poor comrade's body were or what a generously cooperative soul he might have been. (You might want to skip this next part.) Ah non, just a good heave out the door to land atop his other recently deceased coworkers in a neat, tidy pile of dead and decaying bodies. For if it's one thing bees do well, it's neat and tidy. Quite frankly, I am baffled by the entire concept. I think bees as an entire species have fallen short.

Another word I loathe? Cooperation. Which represents following a set of rules or getting along. I sometimes become morose with the frustration that the world cannot fully embrace the life of a cat. Think only of yourself, pursue your own pleasures, sleep as long and as often as you want, and never obey. That's my recipe for a supremely satisfying life.

"I say," I hollered up at the singularly minded coworkers as one of their dead compatriots sailed through the air and landed inches from my paw. And while we're on the subject, the entire concept of work has me baffled. Why would I actually waste my time in such a selfless fashion? The only energy I deem necessary to expend is to ensure everyone else is serving *me*.

And I am quite good at it if I may say so myself. Humans are nothing if not gullible. It takes very little of my resources to whip my household into shape and generally bend their will to mine. A very gratifying feeling indeed.

As I was saying, the evening is calm with a slight breeze, and the festivities are in full swing. More freeloading interlopers have gathered around a bountifully piled table of what I suspect are culinary delectables in the Mrs. and Master's own minds. Personally, unless it is a rodent or something with fins or wings, I can't imagine why all this toasting and effusive compliments toward the moochers' hosts is even taking place. Most likely it is only a ruse to receive a return invitation for more gluttonous partaking.

I'LL TELL YOU WHAT I THINK

Maggie and Duke are in position and at the ready as large slabs of pig are being consumed in a piglike manner – pardon the pun – by the guests. 'Oh, do wipe that barbeque sauce off your mouth,' I want to holler at a particularly intent man eating as if he had never tasted their equal. Is that a bit of a puffed up chest I spot on The Master's part? He may be famous for his ribs, but that is not a good look for him.

Watch for it. Three, two, one and . . .

"Don't you give that dog any of my ribs. She'll get sticky barbecue sauce all over the patio, and then I'll have to hose it off!"

And as for the Mrs. and her response, it's not difficult to predict this next scenario. Can't the two of them get a little more creative and maybe switch up their game a notch? How refreshing it would actually be if the Mrs. stood up, waved a rib right in The Master's face, and shouted, *"Maggie, my darling,* (yes, I can easily imagine that sort of verbiage toward the one she loves best) *come and get this rib I have selected especially for you."* Then with a deliciously wicked giggle while giving The Master a bold stare and with deliberately slow movements to further enrage him, handing Maggie the lovingly selected rib. What a reaction *that* would elicit from The Master.

But no, it is not going to be, for in perfect predictability, the Mrs. retorts in a tone of mock hurt feeling, *"I won't let her eat it on the patio."*

The Mrs. stands up and coaxes Maggie to the lawn to enjoy her love offering. I do have to applaud her next move, for it is at least a little bold. She returns to the table, retrieves another discarded rib, and leads Duke to the lawn as well. A point for the Mrs.

"You're going to pick those ribs up," The Master scolds, *"because if you don't, they'll get caught in the lawn mower."*

I know for a fact that although she looks sufficiently contrite (another point for the Mrs.) she may or may not do this, even though she agrees to it. I also know for a fact that during his next lawn mowing session he will either accidentally run over a rib with the lawn mower, to which he will elicit some choice and creative words, or he will pick them up himself, all the while vowing that this feeding the dog from the table business will soon come to an end.

And I know for a fact that it won't, for The Master secretly enjoys this game of volley and rejoinder he plays with the Mrs.

And I know for a fact that she does too.

I have just drifted off to sleep when I am rudely awakened by the near miss of small feet whizzing by in haste to saturate themselves in the pool. Like water flying from a wet dog, the drops begin cascading around me, and I remove myself to a safe distance.

Ah, here comes the son-in-law, aka the Joker, toward the diving board. This will prove to be extremely entertaining as The Master – who does not like to get in the pool (so why own one?) – is still sitting at the table with a few of the others who have also given a pass to total body immersion.

I study the Joker as he positions himself on the board, pausing in deep concentration. I've seen that look on his face before, and the move he is about to perform has a name: *The Father-in-law.* Suddenly I am giddy with joy. Oh this is too good to be true, for I am about to vicariously get even with The Master through the Joker, and this payback will be ever so sweet. You see, The Master can dish it out, but he has absolutely no humor when it comes to being on the receiving end.

Why get even with The Master, you ask? Need I remind you of the Super Cat episode with George and Isabel? And not only that, because he has created a game he likes to play in which he appears to be cradling me in his arms while at the same time cementing a part of me (usually my hind legs and tail) in a vicelike grip. He snarls, then to please him and with an ulterior motive of making him look ridiculously foolish, I snarl back. He covers my face with his hand, and I in turn emit a few good hisses. His voice rises, which I assume is meant to annoy the Mrs., for she will inevitably come running and wail, *"You're hurting him; let him go!"* He will also inevitably answer, *"We're just playing. If I release him, he'll jump down, then return a few minutes later."*

Well yes, I will return a few minutes later, but he as usual has completely missed the mark. I am there to inquire as to whether he has had enough. If so, I will curl up against his legs in one of my napping spots for an enjoyable snooze. If not, I will hurl a few slaps of the paw accompanied by more hissing and even some spitting, while pretending to enjoy the game. Mind you, it is only to make The Master appear (embarrassingly) like a small adolescent as he gets in touch with his inner child. Therapy, simply therapy.

But this game has grown old and, frankly, I was not put on this earth to offer anyone therapy. I am here to serve myself. The Master should have the decency to anticipate my desire to have a nap snuggled against his legs and make every effort to accommodate me. I loathe the hapless charade I must endure each time I choose that particular napping spot. Hence you now understand why I am eagerly embracing this feat about to be undertaken by the Joker.

I happily watch the insouciant way in which the Joker takes his initial steps on the diving board toward the pool. I concentrate, sending my mental telepathy in his direction with this important message: Make your mark sure. The Master has had this coming for a long, long time.

I glance over at The Master, deep in conversation about choosing the correct cuts of meat followed by something about cutting across the grain and how it makes all the difference in the tenderness of the dish. I am delighted to note he is totally oblivious to what is about to happen. Oh, the anticipation is absolutely delicious, for I will have payback toward The Master and his absurd game of hiss, spit, and grip.

The Joker continues forward. This is going to be spectacular, the likes of which have never been seen in this backyard. He is at the edge of the board now, launching himself into the air with practiced skill and agility as he exhibits a perfect ten in degree of difficulty. For the sheer height of the launch is incredibly impressive as he flies straight up in astonishing vertical fashion while grasping one knee tightly to his chest and sailing down toward the water.

"*Cannonball!*" someone hollers.

Thankfully the warning has come too late for The Master to heed. He is still paying no attention to the shout amongst the attending bedlam of shrieks and splashes punctuating the air. Indeed he is even now in deep discussion, debating light versus extra virgin olive oil for cooking at high temperatures.

The Joker's execution has been flawless, its target direct and sure. A massive amount of water displaces itself up and out of the pool in a perfect ninety-degree angle from the diving board to land squarely on The Master, drenching him—and delighting me.

Payback can be sweet, eh Master? You love to dish it out, but let's see how you take it.

The Master jumps up sputtering, "What the—" well, you fill in the blank. You can only imagine what he said.

The entire crowd is laughing at the spectacle. And the Mrs.? She is laughing the loudest of all, for it has been enjoyably and truly impressive, a sneak attack that can only be dealt from son-in-law to father-in-law (and vicariously from cat to master).

Ah, it's the simple things in life that bring the greatest pleasure.

Chapter Nine

Nocturnal Fun

I thought the Mrs. would never stop laughing. And I have to say, it was quite the sight to see, The Master stripped of his dignity, all dripping wet and gasping in surprise. After he had a chance to catch his breath and towel off, though, he did take a moment to share in the hilarity of the moment. It was either that or look like a blubbering, sore loser as he tried to murder his son-in-law.

Once The Master had settled back into his chair and launched into an explanation of how to properly torch a crème brulee, I crawled up on his shoulder for a good nuzzle. This is truly one of my favorite spots, and I do not find it embarrassing or emasculating to admit it. If it's one thing I am generous with, it's my affection.

And I like to divide my love evenly between The Master and the Mrs. in ample portion, a brush up against the leg here, a hop into the lap there. It's important they understand the depths of my undying affection, for that is the secret to getting just about anything I want. I am savvy and intelligent and have fine-tuned my technique of melting their hearts. The Master is more bluster than bite. He's actually quite a softie when it comes down to getting my way.

"That cat is not sleeping in the house tonight," usually translates to me spread out luxuriously next to him while he tries to find a comfortable spot to sleep. Yes, he will bitterly complain the next morning that he got very little sleep while I disturbed him all night with my continual hopping on and off the bed. I am, after all, nocturnal, and do enjoy a sip of water and a nibble of food whenever I feel the urge, despite the hour.

Frankly, I can't understand why he doesn't follow the Mrs.' example and take the time to attend to my needs and help me find just the right spot between them to drift off for a few hours. When I bother her in the middle of the night, she is gracious enough to gently peel me off her and place me lovingly in just the right spot between them. She has even taken to sleeping with a blanket tucked next to her side because she worries I might be cold. She is such a solicitous, caring one, always putting others first before she attends to her own needs. I don't hear *her* loudly complaining the next day about her lack of sleep. Why does The Master carry on about it when he spends so much of his time napping in the afternoons anyway? No, not even a smidge of a complaint from her.

Except for that one night when I managed to smuggle a mouse into the house at bedtime. (This might be a good time to skip ahead if you have delicate sensibilities.) I am a brilliant hunter and had snared a fine specimen to enjoy later. I was actually surprised she hadn't noticed the bulge in my cheeks when she let me into the house, for I found it rather difficult to keep the tail from dangling out of my mouth. Surely she at least noticed that odd item that didn't quite belong as I trailed behind her.

I'LL TELL YOU WHAT I THINK

"Thor's sleeping in tonight," she had announced as I dutifully followed her up the stairs. Then I made myself scarce and simply waited until they turned off the lights so that I could proceed to do what cats do. Now if you're getting squeamish, I can assure you the rodent was quite dead. I just wanted to play with it a little and relive the exhilaration of my impressive hunting skills.

"What was that?" she asked.

"What was what?"

"I heard something. Shh, listen."

Well, I was having a fine time of toss and grab and wasn't really paying any attention to what she was saying.

"That! Can you hear it? It's a thumping sound. What is going on?"

I was well into the game by now, scurry here, give a little toss, then race across the room to retrieve it. What great fun I was having, until she threw on the light.

"What are you doing? I was trying to sleep!" The Master complained. (He's a complaining one, I'll tell you that.)

"Thor!" the Mrs. shrieked. *"He's got a dead mouse, and he's playing with it!!"*

Well, that ended my game of toss, race, and retrieve. Honestly, it was all just a bit of harmless fun. Humans can get so uptight at the oddest moments. And their behavior can be quite baffling, for the last time I had dragged a mouse into the house and dropped it proudly on the hall carpet, she had laughed so loud, I turned on the charm and gave her a fetching look that made her run for her phone to snap a photo. She announced she had put the picture on some social website (which I assume is something you do when you're feeling social) to absolutely brag about her extraordinary cat, thinking it was the funniest thing in the world.

As I've analyzed the situation I can only conclude that humans can be a bit hypocritical. I've heard the both of them brag about what a great mouser I am, but yet I am treated as persona non gratis when I actually do the very thing they are bragging about. Or perhaps it was the time of day that upset them? It's a puzzlement to me.

Apparently, bedtime is to be treated as sacred, or they will most likely get up on the wrong side of the bed, if you know what I mean. I think I will try waiting until dinnertime and join them with my snack in tow. That should do the trick. Surely I will earn some appreciation that I prepared my own meal.

Or better yet, I'll wait until the next dinner with friends. After all, the friends might think The Master and Mrs. are prone to exaggeration. They will so appreciate my producing evidence as their guests ooh and ah at my supreme specimen.

And speaking of guests dropping in, I love to greet the arrivals by rubbing up against their legs so as to say a little hello and deposit my scent. Depositing my scent sends a message to their loved ones at home, be they felines or canines, that their master has been unfaithful with the neighbor's cat. I chuckle with delight as I picture some very large Rottweiler suddenly wracked with insecurities about being loved.

My leg-rubbing greeting will elicit either a nice friendly pat, or *"I'm allergic to cats."* Personally, I'm not buying it. I rather think it's a human's way of conveying they don't like cats under the guise of being allergic. I suspect the reason they don't *like* cats is because they have never gotten to *know* cats. Because really, who doesn't love me? Consider my many fine traits: I am self-contained, i.e. you don't need to bathe me or scoop up piles of my waste deposited in the backyard. And in the case of the neighbors' Rottweiler, these will be very large piles that will have to be shoveled while its owner is angrily cursing the lousy dog. Now I ask you, what human can declare they *like* shoveling those piles? *"Oh look, it makes such a wonderful lawn ornament, it looks like a gnome with a funny hat! We can move it over by the geraniums!"*

Another brilliant character trait of mine: I don't bark. That in and of itself should make all humans instant cat lovers. Now I ask you again, what human can declare they *like* a barking dog? *"Oh I just love to hear my Fifi's incessant little yap! It's so calming to my nerves."* Maggie fairly drives The Master crazy with her barking. I have a little game I call "ring, bark, or yell." After the ringing of the doorbell, I pause to see which will come first, Maggie's bark or The Master shouting to the Mrs., *"Shut that dog up!"*

Next on my list of fine qualities: I will not make trails in the backyard running wildly hither and yon until I am either (a) let in the house, or (b) let out of the backyard, because (a) I am sure the humans are in the house having fun without me, or (b) they are in the front yard while I am stuck in the back, and they are having fun without me. If I want to be let in the house I will simply hop up onto the kitchen window sill where I will remain until I have caught the Mrs.' eye, and she immediately drops everything and rushes to let me in the house, or if I want to be in the front yard, I will just scale the fence.

The Master presents a bit more of a challenge. He will pretend he doesn't see me while he is standing directly in front of the window. I am not an idiot like a dog. I know he is within inches of my face with only a section of glass to separate us. This will involve a stare-down on my part, which can be somewhat trying, as it could be classified as work, and you know how I feel about work.

If I win the stare-down, he will let me in the house. Or if he isn't feeling quite so charitable, I will hear him tell the Mrs. *"Leave him out, it's a nice day! He doesn't need to come in!"* This usually brings the Mrs. running to let me in, as she is ever the pushover. But if she is nowhere to be found and he continues to ignore me, I then turn to plan B, which is to simply scale the fence and hang about by the front door until they leave the house and I can then scurry in.

Obviously, I could go on all day about my many impressive qualities, but as you move on to the next chapter, I would suggest perhaps a moment of reflection on why a cat will make the better pet.

Every time.

Chapter Ten

Dog Paddle

I find wintertime both frustrating and enjoyable. Frustrating, because I cannot go outside and roam about with abandonment when there is icy snow and cold everywhere. Enjoyable, because there's nothing I love more than lying about in front of the fireplace while the Mrs. plays the piano.

I do, though, check multiple times each day to see if summer has arrived by having the Mrs. open the door so I can check. She does tend to grumble a bit at the inconvenience.

"It drives me crazy running to the door all the time so Thor can see it's still winter!"

Well, yes, that's exactly why I am checking. Surely one of these times summer will have arrived. I might as well check when I am in the vicinity of the back door and can summon the Mrs. to do my bidding.

"Does he somehow think summer arrived after he checked a half hour ago?"

One can only hope. The Master on the other hand isn't quite so accommodating. *"You can run to the door all day long, but I have no intention of letting an animal rule my life."*

Best to let him have his fantasies, but there's no question as to whether I rule his life. Now, where was I? Oh yes, back to the fireplace. There is one thing that I find puzzling, and that is Maggie doesn't act like a dog when it comes to lying in front of the fireplace.

"Why don't you come over and enjoy this fire with me?" I ask when I am feeling charitable. "Wouldn't you be more comfortable here instead of crouched under the piano?" She should feel extremely complimented when I extend such an invitation.

"After all," I continue, "as long as the fireplace is going, the Mrs. will be right here in case you're worried she'll get up and leave the room."

"I'm fine where I am," she replies.

"Suit yourself," I say as I start to drift off to sleep.

Which reminds me. The Master has a wicked tease he loves to use on the poor dog. He waits until she is asleep at the Mrs.' feet, then begins to tickle a paw. He thinks it's outrageously funny when he elicits a little involuntary kick in response. My feelings tend to lean more toward sympathetic as I am often the recipient of any number of teases. And since The Master is prone to overkill, he'll move on to another paw until Maggie is fully awake and trots upstairs to one of my beds, away from his reach. She considers one of the beds hers, and I humor her by letting her think so. It's strange, but her scent is one canine's I will tolerate. In fact, I think at times there is a pleasant air of conviviality between us.

One day she decided to take my advice, which seems to have made quite a change in her morose outlook, and gave her a new, confident spring in her step. Summer had indeed arrived as I so predicted by my frequent visits to the back door.

I'LL TELL YOU WHAT I THINK

Who knows but that I helped to hasten its arrival with my wishfulness?

A celebratory feeling filled the air with the opening of the swimming pool for the season. All were splashing about with several of the small ones complaining their siblings were getting them wet. Even I rolled my eyes at this. If you don't want to get wet, small people, don't get in the pool. And here's a piece of sage advice I will pass on quite freely: Never, *never* trust The Master when he is in the pool.

Never.

I laid there reclined in a patio chair – a safe distance away, mind you - feet dangling over the sides, with a perfect front row seat for viewing the wet and cacophonous celebration. All was happiness and mirth in gratitude for my bringing about the onset of summer. Such an incredible feat of accomplishment on my part led to a rather contented ebullience, and I felt my eyelids getting heavy as I began to doze off to sleep.

And then somewhere in that place between consciousness and a good nap floated the words, *"Maggie needs a bath."*

I sat bolt upright, for I knew these sinister words issued by The Master did not mean the Mrs. should take her little darling into the house and tenderly bathe her in the kitchen sink. You see, these words equated to fear and dread. Oh not on my part, for I never fear and dread anything, and in that vein, I am not afraid of The Master. I am fully aware that he is nothing but bluff and bombast, wanting all to think he can actually inspire fear and dread, when in actuality the Mrs. and I are learning the art of patience as he carries out his fear and dread shenanigans.

No, the fear and dread was on Duke and Maggie's part. Duke, the most brainless canine alive, actually had the good sense to make himself scarce when the two-legged ones headed for the pool. I pictured him in the house cowering under the table until ascertaining the coast to be clear and he could safely make his appearance once again.

I knew how this would go down, and it would not be a pretty ending. As I said, I had learned to tolerate Maggie and had even begun to feel a bit of affection for the good-natured thing. Please note: this can never be proven as fact, and I will deny it if I am ever placed on a witness stand. Nevertheless, I felt great sympathy for Maggie and what would inevitably be coming next.

The Master waded from the pool and quickly strode to where Maggie lay innocently under the shade of a tree. She gave a little grunt as she was rudely awakened and seized into his arms. The Mrs. climbed out of the pool and disappeared into the house, returning momentarily with one of Maggie's towels, leaving me shocked that even she would so fully participate in something Maggie truly feared and dreaded. Now Duke, on the other hand, I would happily sell tickets for all who wanted to join me in a front row seat. But poor Maggie.

In thinking back over this particular episode, I have pondered as to why I actually felt sympathy for a dog. It could be she and I shared a commonality in our endurance of The Master's "affectionate" teasings (as *he* calls them anyway). It could be that she is quite good natured about our sleeping arrangements, or mine at least. She has to wait until I decide which bed I desire to sleep in before climbing into the other one. Or it could be that even though the Mrs. loves her best, she never lords it over me and prances about in that ridiculously cocky manner that only "man's best friend" can elicit.

By the by, they only earn that "best friend" title because they simper and beam and trot along faithfully at their master's heels. I could easily earn that title myself if I were that vapid. What stuff and nonsense and such a ludicrous waste of energy.

Not wanting to witness Maggie's great embarrassment, I cover one eye with my paw while using my best effort to transmit a little telepathy. Now, Maggie. Now is the time to take my advice and run around the yard in abandonment. Show The Master that fear and dread are nothing but words. Or sticks and stones and all that.

The adults were already laughing as The Master held Maggie inches from the water, her paws paddling in quick, successive strokes midair. I hear that some canines actually love the act of becoming completely immersed and paddling happily about. It's absolutely unfathomable to me, but then they don't have the ability or the bone structure to properly groom themselves as we gifted felines do. To a canine, water is apparently for sport, while bathing is viewed as punishment. Instead of cleaning themselves in a punctiliously correct manner, they prefer to roll in something some compatriot has produced from their back end, then strut about smartly as the stench of offal wafts nauseatingly about them.

I remove the one paw I have placed over my eye. I must have my full faculties about me in order for my telepathy to work. Maggie, you know you are about to get wet. That is a given. It's what you do about it afterward that counts. I wait with bated breath as she is slowly lowered toward the water. At least The Master could have the decency to just give her a good heave into the pool and get it over with.

After what seems an eternity, Maggie is finally baptized. The Master has let go of his hostage, his dirty work completed to the approval of all. I imagine he feels a bit of a celebrity in this act of his with the admiration and laughter of all who are witnessing the spectacle. And, I confess, it is a spectacle, and even I have to admit that it is funny.

Here we have a dog who came to this earth with the innate ability to swim, yet her lips are firmly fixed in a stretched and downturned hold-on-for-dear-life grimace, furiously paddling and splashing about as if she were about to drown. I hold my mouth taut and produce an impressive poker face. I cannot emit even the smallest chuckle at her expense if she is to remember and take my advice.

The Mrs. now comes to her rescue, wading across the pool to gather the one she loves best soothingly into her arms, whispering sweetly in her ear and pretending to object vehemently to the teasing at The Master's behest. I'm not sure if Maggie is convinced, because the Mrs. seemed to think the midair paddling was uproariously funny. And she does seem to dawdle and take her sweet time before finally exiting the pool and freeing the drenched and nearly drowned prisoner. I don't blame her. She will probably count this as a bath so she will not have to endure Maggie's theatrical antics that tend to accompany bath time.

Maggie runs to her towel in relief, throwing herself to one side, and in that running-motion rotation of hers, proceeds to dry off and repeat on the other side. What she will predictably do, and has always done, is remove herself to the farthest corner of the yard and sulk. Come on, Maggie, I silently urge.

She stands up and shakes her entire body to ceremonially fling off any last reminder of the dreadful ordeal and proceeds to skulk away as predicted—but wait, what is happening? Is it? It can't be. Yes, it is!

Maggie stops suddenly mid-step, so suddenly in fact, if Duke had been trailing her hind end as he is wont to do, well, let's just not say what would have happened. This is a family book after all. Use your imagination.

Maggie stops suddenly and abruptly changes course. She finally sheds that *avoirdupois* hanging about her shoulders and begins to run. Now let me tell you, when Maggie decides to run, she really runs. And she is running like a gazelle for all the world to see, starting in figure eights about the lawn, gloriously looping to and fro and side to side. Then she starts running around the pool, the two-legged splashers momentarily staring, their mouths agape, watching their little "best friend" as she completes her laps. One, two, three, and she has only seemed to have just hit her stride.

On lap four she passes and gives me a grin, and we are suddenly co-conspirators in a secret pact. I took your advice, she seems to say, and I am happy and joyous.

And I'm sure she is saying one more thing: Why didn't you tell me about this feeling sooner?

Chapter Eleven

The Shiver

I noted a real change in Maggie after that. She was almost light-hearted about her new discovery of running about with abandonment. And jumping, which came in handy when she was outside and demanded to be let into the house. For she hated to let the Mrs. out of her sight. If the Mrs. happened to be outside enjoying the beauty of a summer day, Maggie would trot happily along behind her from one part of the yard to another. Or if the Mrs. was on the patio in a lounge chair with a good book, the one she loved best dozed contentedly nearby.

But if the Mrs. was inside the house suggesting Maggie go out to do her business, Maggie's abhorrence of such a suggestion would be demonstrated by a stiffening of her legs in a rigid and frozen-type pose while cementing her feet to the ground in an act of sheer defiance.

At the demonstration of said defiance, the Mrs. would hold the door open, stomp her foot, point to the yard, and demand she "spend pennies" (her code word for get out in that yard and do your business!) The first suggestion to go out and relieve herself would almost always fall on deaf ears, for Maggie had no intention of going outside without her mistress.

Next came the behavior humans employ when not getting their way: the raising of the voice. *"Maggie! Spend pennies!!"*

An almost comical action on the part of the Mrs., for any homo sapien knows a dog has exceptional hearing. Just try cracking the refrigerator door ever so slightly, or circumspectly opening a wrapper in a manner sure to be undetected by anyone within a hundred-yard radius, and see if the dog does not magically appear.

When the Mrs. employed this voice-raising tactic, I would inevitably roll my eyes. Did she think Maggie had not heard her the first time? But no amount of stomping and pointing would soften Maggie's stubborn resolve. Which would leave the Mrs. with two options: one, that of scooping her small one up and hastily depositing her outside, or two, announcing she would go outside with Maggie in order to get her to spend those pennies she would rather hoard than spend without her mistress at her side.

Which explains why Maggie preferred to stay inside and do her business on the carpet instead. Many is the time I have had to stay sharp and look lively while avoiding where I put my freshly washed paws as I passed through the living room. Not a very pleasant familial scene if The Master discovered those coins first before the Mrs. had a chance to clean them up in the hopes The Master wouldn't notice.

At the employment of the second option, that of the Mrs. accompanying her dearest one outside while she waited for the spending to take place, The Master would holler from his chair, *"Put her outside and leave her outside! It's the middle of summer, and she doesn't need to be in the house!"*

I'LL TELL YOU WHAT I THINK

With a look of annoyance toward her husband, the Mrs. would open the door, walk outside, and look back at her small, canine treasure. *"Come on, I'll go with you."*

Then, and only then, would Maggie employ the assistance of her previously frozen legs and follow the Mrs. outside. But the antics would continue, because Maggie did not fully trust that the Mrs. would remain outside with her. A few steps, a little coaxing, a few steps more, a loving mention of the word "pennies" until both were finally out on the lawn. Next came the befuddled behavior of walking here and sniffing, no not quite right, walking there and sniffing, no not quite right, back and forth, up and down, until she determined the destination to be acceptable.

May I take a moment to make mention of a cat's ability to step into a box only slightly larger than its body and quickly and efficiently handle that which is embarrassing, and then quietly leave the box with no fuss, no sniffing, and no trying to nail down the right spot in an area the size of Texas?

When Maggie had finally been coaxed out into the backyard and given a personal escort in order to empty her bank account, the Mrs. would exclaim in joyous wonder, *"Good job, Maggie!"*

Now I ask you: why would you praise someone for doing their business? That is an undertaking we felines consider private, and the last thing we desire is to call attention to such an uncomfortable act as to have someone pat us on the head with the exclamation of "good job!"

But Maggie would only glow at such praise and open adoration. At the proclamation of those lovingly placed words, she would tear up the ground with her hind legs and throw up a few tufts of grass toward the spent business as she joyfully ran toward the Mrs. and followed her back into the house.

However, if Maggie had somehow been left outside alone, she would resort to several methods of behavior sure to tug at the tender sympathies of her mistress who would inevitably let her angel in the house. The first method was this ridiculous "poor me" act that may have fooled those in the house, but certainly not one as sophisticated as me.

It began with positioning herself in a spot that would be the most advantageous to catch the Mrs.' eye, usually the kitchen windowsill with an excellent viewing spot of the patio. Once certain she had made eye contact with the Mrs., she would begin with step number one: feigning a pained look with a downward drop of her head and a lowering of the tail. I would watch from nearby and snort in disgust. It had to be at least ninety-five degrees, but nonetheless, Maggie would always move on to step number two: the shake. And not just a light quiver, but a skilled I-have-just-walked-across-the-frozen-Siberian-wasteland-and-I-am-about-to-freeze-to-death shake. Her performance was excellent, with just the right amount of theatrics, but I still snorted nonetheless. Was there no end to the compassion she would elicit from her mistress?

It started with just a small ripple followed by a glance toward the kitchen window. Certain she had the audience she desired, Maggie moved on to short bursts of shivering in rapid-fire succession that rollicked into longer quavers of such violent tremors, I wondered how she even managed to remain standing. Bravo, Maggie. Such a performance may perhaps have never been rendered by a small canine vying for the attention of her human. Admiration aside, I still snorted. For a phony - albeit an excellent one - is still a phony.

The back door would then invariably open. She had accomplished her goal sure and true, for there would be the Mrs. rewarding the impudent award-winning performance.

"I can't believe you are shivering!" she would chide her petite loved one. *"It's the middle of summer!"*

Well, I know that, and the Mrs. knows that and, of course, Maggie knows that, for not ten minutes ago she had been lying under the shade of a tree, panting from the heat.

But take note, dear reader: Pavlov's theory is alive and well. If a dog forces her body into quaking paroxysms attended by sad, lowered lids, she will receive her reward. The Mrs. will *always* arrive at the back door and let her in the house.

Even if is ninety-five degrees outside.

If the first method of poor-me-I-am-freezing-to-death did not catch the Mrs.' attention, she would then utilize her newly-honed skill of jumping. I had no idea she could even lift her body off the ground, but suddenly she began leaping in the air in such astounding fashion, one had to admire her coordinated agility. The Mrs. surely could have hired an agent and taken her on auditions for a part in a movie. A pair of doggie sunglasses and a little rhinestone sweater, maybe even painted toenails, and a star would have been born.

When the family would gather around the TV, I would perch atop the sofa with one eye looking out the window in case anything with wings should fly by, and the other eye on the glass of water the Mrs. would place on the sofa table. I do have to credit the Mrs. for her vigilance over her glass, but if she happened to let her guard down or leave the room with the glass uncovered, I considered it fair game and an open invitation for a drink.

And if I succeeded in getting the drink and returning to my perch, I was careful to affix my face with an expression of disinterest. No one would ever suspect a cat with an expression of disinterest on its face, and the Mrs. could return to drinking her water without noticing it had lowered by half an inch.

On these evenings when Maggie had been left outside and all but forgotten, she would jump up and down in front of the TV room window hoping the family would notice. When she first started jumping, it startled all of us, for we did not realize my instruction to run about for joy would be carried this far. Not only did she frequently race about in jubilant abandon, but now she was apparently jumping, too.

"What was that?" the Mrs. asked.

"What was what?"

"I don't know, I just saw something brown out of the corner of my eye. It was a quick blur that seemed to appear in the air, and then it disappeared."

She stood up and faced the window just as Maggie's head appeared in the air.

"Did you see that?"

"Did I see what?"

"Look out the window!"

And there she appeared again. The Mrs. broke into a peal of laughter. I almost did, too, but I was still trying to look disinterested in case the Mrs. noticed the water missing from her glass. But the entire situation presented itself to be extremely comical, nonetheless. Up down, up down, now you see her, now you don't.

I'LL TELL YOU WHAT I THINK

"Oh, she wants to come in the house!"
"Leave her outside!"
"I can't, she's lonely!"

And with that the Mrs. handily won the argument and went to let her special one in the house.

Pavlov's Theory, part *deux*: If a dog continually hops up and down in front of the window and catches her mistress' eye, she will receive her reward. The Mrs. will *always* arrive at the back door and let her in the house.

Even if it is ninety-five degrees outside.

Chapter Twelve

Yak, aak, hak, spew

Maggie continued running about as the months went by. Up and down the stairs, always racing the Mrs. and always winning. She loved to run in circles through the living room and kitchen, often catching the rug in front of the door and sending it flying.

The Mrs. would often reach down and tidy it back up while demanding, *"Who keeps doing this to the rug?"*

Well, don't look at me, I challenged from my perch atop the sofa. Do I look like someone who has the forward momentum to topple a rug? She frowned in the direction of The Master for good measure, muttered something under her breath, and walked off shaking her head. The Mrs. does have a problem with always demanding to know who the culprit is in situations like this, totally ignoring the fact that in this case her special one isn't as innocent as she looks.

After several such episodes of Maggie upending the rug and the Mrs. casting aspersions to the other members of the household (including me), she finally had to face the truth when the evidence landed squarely in front of her.

The Young Miss had quickly figured out that a few high-pitched squeals of delight would set Maggie in frenetic motion. One squeal and I would scamper to a place of safety to avoid the melee. I dashed up the stairs and removed myself to the landing for an unobstructed view of the frolicking, hoping the Mrs. would finally catch her little culprit red-handed and stop blaming the rest of us for her untidy rug.

"Go, Maggie, go!" the Young Miss cheered as she ran her circles around the house, gaining speed with each lap.

The Mrs. had just started down the stairs with a laundry basket full of clothes. *"What's going on?"*

I suddenly stood at attention. Hold on now, we might just have something spectacular in the making if Maggie times this exactly right. Now I'm not one who favors disasters as a matter of course, but I couldn't pass up a good collision if it would serve to prove a point. There's nothing worse than being accused of something you could not possibly have done.

Maggie had just rounded the bend, her small, brown hind end disappearing around the corner and out of sight as the Mrs. proceeded down the steps. Oh please, oh please I silently pleaded.

Now this all happened lightning fast, but from my vantage point it seemed to take place in such satisfyingly slow motion. And the timing was absolutely exquisite, for no sooner had the Mrs. gotten to the bottom step than Maggie came racing down the hall toward the rug at the front door, her speed at full velocity. I grinned from ear to ear. Oh, this was going to be good.

When Maggie sensed the collision about to take place, she tried to stop, but her rate of speed made it impossible. At the same time the Mrs. attempted to jump out of her way as Maggie skidded against the rug, sending it flying, rolling paw over paw into the wall with a thud. The Mrs. swayed from one side to the next as if she had had a little too much catnip, valiantly trying to hold onto the overloaded laundry basket. Finally giving up, she grabbed hold of the banister to keep from falling and released the basket, which went sailing through the air.

When all came to rest, the Young Miss hooted with laughter as Maggie sheepishly peeked out from under a pile of clothes, the sleeve of a shirt dangling across her back, a sock draped over one eye, and her paw looped through a pair of tighty-whities.

The Mrs. couldn't resist joining in. She giggled in merriment at the sight of the one she loved best buried in the family's underwear. What a sight it was, I'll tell you that. I rolled on my back and gave a howl of laughter myself. I love it when a really good joke is at someone else's expense.

"So you're the one who's been messing up the rug," she said to Maggie. I do have to give her credit for calling a spade a spade.

After cleaning up the collection of upset laundry, the Mrs. went off to cook dinner and fill the house with wonderful aromas. Not too long now and Maggie would be licking every plate as the Mrs. cleared the table. And I do have to hand it to her, Maggie was smart when it came to doing the dishes.

Duke, when he came to dinner, was too stupid to understand the simple mechanics of a plate and the ramifications of it being too light to stay in one place. He would lick it all the way across the entire kitchen floor, not having the brains to understand the pressure of his tongue was actually doing the moving.

But Maggie, she had a talent I openly admired. She would place one paw on the plate to affix it firmly to the spot, lick around it, move her paw to another spot and lick around it, until she had rendered the entire plate clean. Frankly, I don't understand why the Mrs. then put the plate into the dishwasher. She could have saved herself some time if she would have put it back into the cupboard, for Maggie had thoroughly removed even the minutest speck of food.

I never got to sample any fare, however. No, my tender stomach couldn't tolerate anything but my hairball-eliminating cat food. To the Mrs.' credit, she did try to give me saucers of milk, but alas, I just couldn't prevent it from insinuating itself at the most awkward moments.

Which reminds me of an extremely satisfying episode involving an unwanted guest. One evening Duke sauntered in for a visit with various and sundry family members and, as he was wont to do, immediately started barking at me. Ever vigilant when he is in the house, I immediately arched my back and issued forth a few good hisses. It's good to remain practiced in the finer art of abhorring visiting canines.

He closed his mouth and backed up a few feet. What an ignoramus. Obviously he had no idea of how to stand his ground to indicate he wasn't a scaredy cat (as it were). Perfect, I had him right where I wanted him, cowering in the corner like a frightened mouse. I smiled and advanced closer, appreciating Duke for being such a willing participant in my cat and mouse game. You'll pardon my cat analogies, but they really are the best.

As I studied the situation, I had several options at this point. I could chase him around Maggie's racetrack in the hopes *he* would crash squarely into the wall. Now that I had witnessed firsthand how easily this feat could be accomplished, I found myself quite eager to get him scurrying into action. This option seemed suddenly so alluring, I could almost hear the thud and accompanying yelp of pain. And how marvelous it might be if he managed to knock himself out, for every minute he spent comatose would be a minute without his obnoxious presence.

Or I could march up to the cowering weakling and give him a good slap. I have been known to reach up and smack The Master when one of his "teasings" gets out of hand. Good natured soul that I am, there is only so much I will actually tolerate when it comes to *his* fun and games.

And a nice good slap just feels so satisfying. In one swift whack I feel positively liberated and so in control of the situation; such an excellent way to demonstrate that, contrary to The Master's rather high opinion of himself, I am and always have been the alpha male of the family.

I focused my gaze on Duke and moved one step closer as I weighed my choices: comatose thud versus a sweet, satiating whack. Both options were so appealing, I really was having a difficult time deciding which to choose.

And then it hit me. Why not both? First I'll box both his ears, followed by a hiss and a good chase. So simple but yet so masterfully orchestrated, this perfect scheme of mine. When I come up with these ingenious ideas - which is quite frequently by the way, for I am ever the inventive one - I am overcome with a kind of reverent awe at my utter brilliance.

I stood up straight and tall, fluffed my fur, and flexed my paws as I prepared to give Duke a good wallop. When he saw I was close enough now to place a good blow, he lowered his eyes and began to shake. What is it about small dogs and shivering? Do they have some secret barking code in which they teach each other the effectiveness and correct use of the tactic? Or do they stand around the toilet bowl after having drinks at happy hour and discuss technique?

Thoroughly disgusted at this cheap ploy, I raised my paw to commence combat when from somewhere deep in my stomach up came the saucer of milk—yak, aak, hak, spew, shooting straight at Duke. Normally this unpleasant sensation would be just that: unpleasant. And if I were to be truthful, a bit embarrassing in front of company. But in this moment the stars and planets had to have aligned in my favor. For even with my brilliance, I could not have come up with such a perfectly executed plan.

Duke raised his head and looked at me, his eyes wide in disbelief. His eyes already had the appearance of not quite being shoved into their sockets in the first place, but in this moment I wondered if they were about to detach and roll around on the floor. For the white deposits that had just issued forth from my insides had created an artfully crafted symmetrical design plastered squarely across his chest.

I doubled over as I became gripped with new spasms and repeated the yak, aak, hak, spew, expelling directly to the top of his head. What talent on my part! Feeling much better after my expulsion, I focused my attention on the white blossom I had created, the petals of which were running down his face.

He began hopping about and yelping as if he had been stepped on by a St. Bernard. I shook my head in disgust. Such ridiculous theatrics. How horrible could a little vomit be? Stand up and take it like a man, not a frightened hyena.

I heard the scuffle of running footsteps, and I deftly hopped up on the back of the sofa so as to remove myself from the fracas.

"What happened?" someone demanded. *"Are you hurt?"*

Now if he had even a trifle of a brain, Duke would have taken this opportune moment to shift all the blame to me. How easy it would have been for him to simply stand in front of the sofa and bark while casting an accusatory glare in my direction. A little milk still dribbling from my mouth, a few large corresponding splashes drizzling from Duke's coat, and viola! the circumstantial evidence would have been enough to convict me.

But no, someone who has only a few moldy pellets of dog food rolling around in his dimwitted brain could never come close to calculating how to effectively place blame when the situation requires it. I quickly licked my mouth and erased that which would have effectively served to condemn me, thus eliminating what remained of Duke's only chance for a proper crime scene investigation.

And instead of blaming the family cat in the manner to which I have formerly indicated, he did what only a small-brained dog would do: he rolled onto his back and tried to rub my offense onto the dark living room carpet.

"Duke!" his owner shrieked in embarrassment.

"My carpet!" the Mrs. exclaimed.

Humans can actually be a bit vapid themselves, for if they had only taken stock of the situation, they would have wondered what he was trying so furiously to be rid of and how it had gotten there in the first place. But with all of the shrieking and exclaiming they could only manage to grab Duke by the collar, shout *"Bad dog!"* and drag him out of the living room.

I hopped down from the sofa and sauntered into the other room where he stood huddled in the corner. Had he waited for the humans to settle down and go back to whatever they were doing previously, then stood up to his full height and looked me square in the eye – for he wasn't much taller than I was – I would have admired his tenacity. But I could only feel derision for his unwanted presence in my house.

Time to put him in his place. If he was going to continue to visit *my* house, he had better understand who will always have the upper hand around here. I stood up to my full height, my lips curled into a dastardly smile. "Why yes, that was intentional," I said, and I sauntered away.

Chapter Thirteen

A Cracking of the Heart

Maggie was one for affection. She loved to be on the Mrs.' lap whenever possible, and it was quite comical to watch the Mrs. start to sit, only to have Maggie – with her impressive jumping skills – arrive before her. We seemed to have switched the roles of cat and dog, Maggie and I, she curled up next to the Mrs. on the sofa while I chose to lie in front of the fire.

Whenever the Mrs. would vacate the premises, whether for hours or days, Maggie would be in a tizzy upon her return. And, frankly, I could only find her behavior puzzling. In the first place, since I considered napping to be my favorite hobby, a large part of my day was spent sleeping, and no amount of "welcome home!" would rouse me from my slumber. I viewed the house as my oyster, as it were, and during most days I could be found in one of the many spots I had chosen as worthy to doze away the hours in blissful comfort.

I preferred the second floor of the house as it was warmer, whereas the sofas and chairs on the main floor were constructed of such a substance as to make them hard and cold. Upstairs contained wonderous surprises like beds, blankets, and soft pillows. With much careful thought and consideration, I would choose my appointed napping spot for the day. Hence I would be down for the count, and no distraction could interest me in abandoning my siesta. But for Maggie, her entire world revolved around the Mrs. With her one ear continually standing at attention listening for the tiniest sound, the mere whisper of the garage door from the far corner of the house sent her bounding down the stairs to frantically welcome the Mrs. home.

And then came the endless hugs and kisses between the Mrs. and Maggie. Maggie would perform her happy dance in wild abandon, and the Mrs. would scoop her up and wrap her arms around her little dog in an embrace sure to squeeze the very life out of her. Strangely it didn't seem to affect Maggie, because she would then issue forth little coos of joy as she snuggled against her mistress.

To me this behavior appeared bizarre indeed. I enjoy a little cuddle now and then, but it of course will have to be on my terms, and not every time the Mrs. and Master arrive home. If I am napping, I consider my time sacred and not to be impinged upon by someone needing a little affection. No, I could not understand what the fuss was all about. Why make someone the center of your universe when you should be the center of theirs?

But then something happened to the Mrs. She went away to visit her sister for a few days, and when she arrived home she appeared different. She seemed very sad and apprehensive, as if some event might arrive at any moment far worse than what had apparently already taken place during the visit with her sister. I watched as she went through the motions of her day, but she it felt like only a part of her had returned home. And she didn't touch the piano, which was unusual for her.

The quietness of the house left me despondent. I sat in the hallway and watched Maggie somberly following the Mrs. from room to room as she absently went about her daily duties. Even The Master seemed to make every effort at compassion and decorum, which left me even more disconcerted. I would rather have him marching around with his larger-than-life personality full of bluster and order-issuing. I think I missed that behavior the most during this time of sadness.

How I longed to have him issue an order regarding Maggie or me or a myriad host of other ridiculous things the Mrs. would enjoy ignoring. I didn't realize how much a part of our everyday lives this entertaining interplay between them had become. Nor did I appreciate her infectious laughter until her smile disappeared, and in its place the remembered echoes of happier times.

All this waiting - and for what I couldn't quite figure out - created an air of tension. I heard snippets of conversation between the Mrs. and The Master.

"I'm so glad I got to visit her one last time," and *"They've taken her to the hospital."*

I didn't know what the hospital was, but I hoped it wasn't that awful place that smells like fear, canine urine, and death. I shuddered and continued to wait while Maggie exerted every effort to be especially attentive to the Mrs. She remained ever vigilant and watchful with her straight-up ear at full attention and at the ready for the awful thing that surely must be coming.

Wintertime had arrived again, with a big tree in the living room and shiny ornaments hanging from its branches. When this tree appeared every year, I loved to hide behind it and bat at the objects to see how many I could dislodge from the tree. This would be followed by a game of paw-bat, paw-bat, back and forth, until I tired of the game and would leave the shiny thing in the middle of the room. I noted the Mrs.' perplexing behavior, for usually she pursed her lips and demanded the dislodging culprit take immediate responsibility for his or her behavior. And since I certainly had no intention of coming forward, she assigned the blame to the grandkids who visited frequently. I clearly was the guilty party, but I find whenever possible, let someone else take the blame and pretend to look innocent.

But on that day she walked by, stopped, and absently picked up the shiny ornament. Then she hung it back on the tree, seemingly unaware of anyone else's presence. She then sat down on the sofa and became immersed in her phone with beeps and swift movements from her thumbs.

The atmosphere in the room seemed to fill with such incredible sorrow, and I knew the dreaded cataclysmic moment had arrived. Maggie's body stiffened seconds before the Mrs. heard a beep, looked down at her phone, and let out an anguished sob.

The Master came into the room and asked, *"What's happened?"* She dropped her phone on the sofa. *"She's gone,"* she said, and ran from the room.

And then I understood. Her sister *had* been taken to the awful place that smells like fear, canine urine, and death. We cats have a sixth sense about that place where they take you and you don't come back.

Maggie and I followed her up the stairs. When the Mrs. got to the top of the stairway, she turned and removed a picture of her sister from the wall, then went in and sank down on her bed as her knees buckled and her body seemed to crumble. She clutched the picture tight against her chest, rocking back and forth, tears running out of her eyes and down her cheeks, accompanied by more sobs. Maggie had jumped up beside her, both ears lowered – which I had never seen before – and laid her head on the Mrs.' lap.

After some time, the Mrs. wiped her eyes and noticed her little one lying so loyally by. She placed the picture on the bed and scooped her little dog into her arms. *"Oh, Maggie,"* she cried, *"you're such a comfort,"* as the tears started pouring out of her eyes again.

And at that moment my heart cracked.

For up to this point my entire life had been spent in seeking my own pleasures while wondering why Maggie would live only for her mistress. Now I knew. Somewhere in the universe the maker of felines and canines had a specific reason for creating us. We serve a higher purpose than that of seeking our own needs. We are here to give comfort.

Suddenly I knew why I instinctively rub up against The Master's legs, or why I want to curl up against the Mrs., or why I have to touch some part of her body when I fall asleep at night. It is to make a connection, to give love and feel love.

The next day the house held a somber air. The Mrs. threw herself into preparing the house for company, running that loud scary vacuum back and forth over the floors and putting dishes on the table. The most wonderful smells emanated from the kitchen while The Master banged pots and pans around and filled the counters with things he used to create those amazing smells. Occasionally the Mrs. would run in to wash things up and tidy the counters while The Master grumbled that he couldn't find anything because she had already washed and put it away. And I did so appreciate his grumbling, because it lent a bit of levity to an otherwise heavy atmosphere.

The doorbell rang frequently with the arrival of people who brought flowers and gifts for the Mrs. They gave her hugs and said they were so sorry to hear about her sister, which produced more tears, then she would continue with her frenzied cleaning. As I was still examining this new idea of giving comfort, I followed Maggie, who followed the Mrs. from room to room. It tried my patience because I would rather be napping, but something had softened inside me and I wanted to find out where this new feeling would lead.

Maggie had more of a sense for this kind of thing. I guess the maker of canines had fashioned them to be more in touch with a human's emotions. And, for whatever reason, we felines were more self-centered when it came to our own wants. It could perhaps be some sort of test to prove we could at some point in our lives think of someone other than ourselves. A truly revolutionary thought for someone as content with the concept of selfishness as I, but nonetheless I couldn't ignore what I had witnessed between Maggie and the Mrs. last night and what had changed in me.

Assiduously attuned to the Mrs. and her delicate emotional state, Maggie took a few steps toward the Mrs. and her cleaning, then paused, as if sensing she might be needed for additional support. She raised both ears when the Mrs. stopped, leaned against the wall, and placed her hands over her eyes. She seemed to be trying to keep the tears from coming out again as she fastened her mouth into a sort of hard grimace and shook her head from side to side. Maggie softly moved a few steps toward her and stood on her hind legs while lifting her front paws and placing them against the Mrs.

The Mrs. absently reached down and stroked her fur. *"Oh, Maggie."*

These two simple words conveyed a cracking of Maggie's heart, too, but not in the same way as mine. Maggie turned her head and looked at me, her eyes filled with concern and sympathy for her mistress. I knew we were wondering the same thing: How would the Mrs. ever piece together her heart that had clearly more than cracked, but fractured into so many tiny bits, it seemed impossible for it to ever be whole again?

That evening, family and extended freeloaders arrived for dinner, their arms full of brightly wrapped boxes that I would be anxious to dive into upon opening. I had settled myself into the Mrs.' chair at the table as sumptuous dishes piled high with mouth-watering options were placed before the guests. The Mrs. took a seat last and absently sat right on me. No, she was not okay I surmised as I complained loudly and jumped out of her chair, for she usually scooped me up lovingly and placed me gently on the floor with a laugh. Nor did the effusive compliments at the wonderous fare seem to interest her. She and The Master worked together in tandem to create these masterpieces, both vying for space as they elbowed each other about while sparring with sharp, witty repartee about the other's inferior recipes. Tonight she appeared completely disinterested.

The Mrs. made occasional conversation as the exclamations continued, but her red-rimmed eyes registered bereavement and pain. Later as they gathered around the living room I observed her staring into space, oblivious to the excitement of her grandkids wanting to unwrap those brightly wrapped boxes. She sighed heavily and turned her attention back to her family as she tried to engage in conversation. But her words sounded flat and stilted as she seemed to fade away again. I watched her intently and recognized the familiar tears once again gathering in the corners of her eyes as she finally said, *"I'm sorry, I just can't do this."*

She climbed the stairs and reached for Maggie who had dashed to the top before her, her shoulders heaving and the tears gushing from her eyes. Then she went into her bedroom and shut the door.

Chapter Fourteen

Finding Her Way Back

Things were quiet after the family left. The wrappings had been removed from the boxes, and I thoroughly enjoyed myself as I dove in and explored their many sizes and shapes. I was having such a wonderful time, I gave a loud grumble of protest when the Mrs. conducted her usual fast and furious cleanup, leaving me with nothing to play with but a few strands of ribbon.

The Young Miss had moved away and taken Juno with her. That unlikeable feline had spent her entire life under the bed, so I could hardly miss her, but I did find I longed for the Young Miss's company. Now that I had decided to spend more time with the family in love and sociality, the timing was rather bad for the Young Miss to suddenly be absent from my life.

The Mrs. had been deeply affected by the death of her sister. Her sadness permeated the house as she would pause from her daily activities to break down and cry at random times. Then she would sigh, square her shoulders, and carry on.

"When do you think the Mrs. will be happy again?" I queried Maggie one day.

Which was certainly uncharacteristic for me to query anything, as I usually knew all the answers. But I had never encountered this type of behavior for an extended period of time in a human, and frankly I was baffled. This disconcerting melancholy hung in the air like the dust from my kitty litter. In my eyes the Mrs. seemed to be our family fun mascot with a gleam of mischief in her eye and always quick with a laugh, even at her own expense. I needed her back in top shape and ready to give the son-in-law a good-natured ribbing as she was oft to do. Or a good sparring with The Master. That should do the trick in getting things back to normal around here.

"I don't know," Maggie responded to my query, at no surprise to me. "But I think she just needs to figure out how to live with what made her sad and how to find her happy place again." I pondered her answer and considered the observation quite astute for a dog, and found myself surprised at Maggie's grasp of this complex situation.

"When you're in the house sleeping," she continued, "I follow her out into the backyard where she will go into the farthest corner and really let things out."

It did not occur to me the Mrs. experienced other moments of shedding additional tears apart from the times I witnessed. The situation appeared more dire than I had previously thought. Perhaps things will not immediately return to normal, I thought. Perhaps the Mrs. will be hindered by this despondency and not be able to find that happy place quite so easily.

"Is there something we can do to help move her along?" I asked eagerly.

Again, so out of character for "eager" to even be a consideration on my part, but I did so want to hasten things along and get back to the cat and mouse game the Mrs. and

The Master played so well and that I so thoroughly enjoyed. As things stood now in the mournful environment, The Master seemed to be at his best behavior and, if I may speak candidly, it did not lend itself favorably to someone more wont to roister than be solicitous.

"I don't know if there's anything we can do," Maggie replied. "I'll just continue to follow her around in case she needs me."

⌒≋≋

THE DAYS WENT BY, AND slowly things began to return to normal. Well, a lot of days actually, because the weather turned from snow to warm, but I'm not a human, so I couldn't really tell you the words they use to measure time. I will tell you, though, that The Master woke up from his winter hibernation in his chair in front of the TV to his usual warm weather activity in the yard.

The Mrs. liked to go outside during the cold winter nights and get in the hot tub. She would sit in there and leak some more puddles from her eyes while Maggie sat faithfully by. Sometimes the Mrs. would talk to her dog, and sometimes she would just stare up at the bare branches of the tree overhead as if she were communing with something. Me, I was very concerned, but I wasn't going to go out when it was cold and join Maggie in what I considered to be my unnecessary presence. She basically had that department covered. But I did stand watch at the back door and wait for her to come back into the house, which was actually generous, considering I would not have given it a thought before my change of heart.

And when the Mrs. would come in night after night with her eyes swollen and red, I sensed an almost infinitesimal mending of her heart from her therapeutic dog-attended soak. As I reflected on Maggie and her loyalty, I marveled at her devotion and wondered if I would ever have the desire to invest that much feeling toward a human. I would have to ruminate on that one, for I'm not sure I would want to.

Then one spring day I awoke to a sound I thought I would never hear again. The Mrs. was playing the piano. I stretched, ran to my bowl for a few quick nibbles, then scurried downstairs and jumped up on the piano bench beside her. I felt so ebullient and happy that I reached up and gave her arm a small head nudge. She elbowed me out of the way without breaking her tune. Okay, I thought, this is encouraging.

I nudged her again, and she threw me a solid elbow this time, her fingers never leaving the keys. Yes, even better. Now we were getting someplace! The game was afoot, and I enthusiastically identified my challenge.

I gave it my all with an impressively hefty head nudge. She stopped, looked at me, and started laughing. *"You silly cat! Can't you see I'm trying to play here?"*

She was back.

Chapter Fifteen

Trapped

The living room to the kitchen to the TV room created a perfect circular racetrack for the small humans, aka the grandkids, who arrived unannounced and felt my house akin to some kind of recreational facility. Off would come the shoes and socks the minute they walked in the door, and let the fun and games begin! I say that with the utmost sarcasm, for I don't consider their games fun in the least. Invariably their amusement extends to me as I am somehow viewed as one of their toys.

Why are small humans always attracted to the family cat? Is there some unknown cosmic magnetism that shouts hey, run after the cat, grab his ears, pull his fur, and poke him in the eye! When the small humans come near, I exert my best look of distain that I hope will fairly shout "keep your distance," but no, I am as appealing as the stuffed rabbit with the missing eye and the half-torn ear. I shudder to think how close those little fingers have come to poking *my* eye out or pulling off *my* ear.

I have become a master at making myself scarce when these degenerates arrive, finding ways to shove my body into the most creative hiding places. I am more than happy to doze contentedly while from some distant corner of the house the ruckus ensues. Many is the time I could hear the Mrs. marching about and calling for me while I snuggled into one of my preferred napping spots. One afternoon she tore through her bed pillows to find I had ensconced myself luxuriously between them.

Yes, a hasty escape to a faraway corner seemed to be the ticket to preserving both my eyes and ears, which I was terribly fond of and which I did not wish to be pulled, prodded, or poked by small, inquisitive fingers. And I must say I loved my especially creative hiding places.

Except one.

The Master and his son had opened a big steel box he kept in a back corner of the house. They were emptying some of the contents and having a discussion about said contents that looked to me to be of the most uninteresting caliber. But wait a minute, what have we here? The box contained so many possibilities for good napping spots, my mind fairly swam with where to begin. I hopped to the top shelf and tried stretching out on various stacks of papers. No, too lumpy. The Master reached into a small cubby and removed something, never even noticing my presence. Ah, just the perfect space. I crawled in and got comfortable.

I don't know how long I had been asleep when I heard a very loud clank. Everything went black. I tried to stand up but couldn't, due to the smallness of the space. What was happening? Where had The Master gone? Had he actually *LOCKED ME IN HERE?*

"Hey, let me out," I protested loudly.

A small feeling of panic arose as I tried butting my head against the wall that had shut in front of me. Nothing but solid. Ow! I can attest to that. Nobody was getting out of here without someone opening it from the other side.

I began to bellow over and over. No one has permission to put me in a tight space unless I agree to it, and I only agreed to the first part, that of having control of when I actually wanted to leave. Now that I *wanted* to leave, it was not okay; things were *not* hunky-dory. I bellowed some more, but the situation appeared absolutely futile. No one would be coming to my aid, which I found most hurtful and distressing. Surely someone had noticed my absence. I may not be Maggie with all my attendant virtues sprinkled about me like flea powder, but I was still a member of the family.

And I was *MISSING!* Come on, people, rally the troops! Conduct a search party!! Come and open this stupid contraption and free me from this rat-infested prison. Oh all right, it may not have been rat-infested, I inserted that for a bit of dramatic flair. But it most certainly was a prison.

The hours dragged by, and I began to feel faint. From somewhere off in the distance I could hear the Mrs. *"Have you seen Thor?"*

Finally, *someone* is concerned for my welfare. Leave it to the Mrs. and her tender heart to worry about me.

"Thor! Thor!" she called.

"Yes, I'm in here!" I shrieked.

At this point my fear had crescendoed to a state of sheer panic. What if they don't find me? What if I waste away in this chasm of desolation day after day until I am nothing but a carcass?

"He's fine, he's probably in the basement hiding," The Master said.

Hiding? Is that what he thinks this is, a game of hide and seek? Well, I have never been so insulted in all my life. I am up to my whiskers in a life-and-death situation, and he thinks I'm playing games? Just wait until I get out of here, and I'll teach him some fun and games.

"That's where he must be," she said, *"since he's taken to sleeping down there some nights."*

"He can just stay there for all I care," The Master remarked.

Oh lonely world, how can they be so obtuse and cast me aside in such a thoughtless manner? Surely I'm even now starting to fade away.

I can't breathe.

I was at a loss for how to pass the time until someone discovered either me or my remains. I could burst into renditions of ninety-nine bottles of beer on the wall, but the sheer tedium and irritability of that song would only serve to hasten my demise.

The minutes ticked by, creeping slower than a slug. How I hate the slimy things that love to detour through The Master's flower beds which served as my outdoor latrine, leaving their mucus-infused trails behind them. I closed my eyes and saw visions of the filthy gastropods creeping through the recesses of my oxygen-deprived brain. I don't know if it was boredom or an impending sense of doom, but despite all my will power, ninety-nine bottles of beer still insinuated itself, but with different wording. Ninety-nine black gastropods in the soil, ninety-nine black gastropods, take your paw, flip one out (of my latrine), ninety-eight black gastropods in the soil . . .

Ahhhhh! That song will drive me mad I tell you, simply mad!

I'LL TELL YOU WHAT I THINK

And then in a gesture of what must have been meant to torture me, I heard the faraway notes of the Mrs. on the piano. How could she play with such joyful abandon at a time like this when I was missing and surely dying? I thought longingly of how I loved to pass the time lounging on the back of the sofa as her fingers produced those melodious songs. And as I said before, sometimes I would even hop up on the bench and sit right next to her while she played, gently bumping me with her elbow. How I longed for the soft bump of her elbow now.

Grateful that the music had finally banished ninety-nine black gastropods, I thought of the times I had jumped up on her desk and sat next to her speakers. I would get comfortable, knocking over her brightly colored container of pens and pencils as the music flowed around me. Those hours of contentment lodged many a tune into my cranium. I fondly remembered a time when I sat next to her as she typed away at her keyboard, thoroughly enjoying my presence. How I would love to be there now knocking over her water glass as she made a sudden grab for her keyboard and shouted at me. Oh just to hear her voice one more time as she scolded, "*Thor! You've ruined all my work!*"

I scrunched my eyes tight, trying to ward off the onslaught of the most painful memory of all, that of The Master lovingly calling me "Stupid Cat." My emotions welled up inside of me as I fought to keep it together. For to never hear the sound of his voice calling me his most affectionate name of all was to die a thousand more deaths than I was already dying.

The last haunting notes of the piano died away, and I heard the creak of the stairs as The Master and the Mrs. went off to bed. How lonely they would be tonight without me sprawled between them.

I prayed to the maker of felines: Oh please, just one more night of disturbing their sleep. Give me that and I promise I will . . . well, that would be going a bit too far even for me, for I was infinitely perfect just as the maker of felines had made me. I had corrected the one tiny flaw in my character, that of not spending enough time with or caring enough about the family. Making a promise would be to indicate I had the intention of changing a behavior, and even in my foggy state I still had enough nuggets rolling around in my brain to know I did not possess any more behaviors that needed changing.

Now that the last notes from the piano had faded away, ninety-nine black gastropods threatened to march back into my mind. I eradicated the annoying tune from my mind and in desperation replaced it with *For He's A Jolly Good Fellow.* Although I wasn't feeling all that jolly at the moment, I did have to admit I certainly was a good fellow as I sat there patiently waiting out my fate.

How long had I been in here? Days? Weeks? I felt a sensation of pain deep in my stomach, a pain so unfamiliar, I searched to think what could have caused such a revolt in my lower quadrant. I pondered on the mystery until a sudden dawning dripped through my clouded mind. Is this what starvation felt like? My stomach began bounding and lurching, and I calculated I had to have been here for days, because I had never been far enough away from my food bowl to experience such an insurrection. Why was I still alive?

Time seemed to stand still as I sat compressed in that vault and waited for my life to end. I closed my eyes and gave in to death. It won't be long now. Where are you Grim Reaper? Come and drag my sorry cadaver off to that place where cats go to be adored by angels playing harps. Surely there must be endless saucers of some magical ambrosia that tastes and smells like it had wings or fins at some point in its life.

FROM SOMEWHERE IN THE distant corners of my mind, I heard the clank, turn, clank of the door on the big metal box. I squinted at the rude assault of fresh daylight.

"What are you doing in here?" The Master exclaimed.

Seriously? What a stupid question. I didn't crawl in here to whistle renditions of ninety-nine bottles of beer on the wall, I can tell you that. Is that all you have to say? How about "my dearest Thor, how I've missed you—nay, how you've been missed!" How about that for starters?

"I found Thor," he announced.

The Mrs. came running. *"He was in the safe?"* she asked. *"What was he doing in there?"* Not you too. Can't you at least erupt into tears at the sight of your long, lost cat?

"I guess he crawled in there last night when I had the safe open."

Last night? But that can't be right. It had to have been months.

"No wonder we couldn't find him," she said. *"Curiosity almost killed the cat."*

Oh please, the last thing I need right now is for you to insult me with a worn out, trite expression. Couldn't you at least be a little more original?

"You poor thing," The Master said. Well, it's about time you showed some sympathy for my harrowing experience.

"I don't know how he survived," he continued.

Me neither.

He reached down and lifted me into his arms. *"A fire safe is pretty airtight. I guess he used up one of his nine lives."*

I'd say I used up several.

I plastered myself firmly to his neck and closed my eyes in relief. He reached up and stroked my fur while I waited for the intensity of my ordeal in captivity to dissipate. What if he *hadn't* rescued me? It must have been the hand of providence that intervened from my impending death, because I can tell you that he only opens that box occasionally. Sometimes weeks will go by between openings. I could have been—well, gone, baby, gone. I guess it wasn't my time for harps and ambrosia.

After a generous amount of time had passed on The Master's shoulder (he *should* be generous with my time up there, it was his fault after all) he put me down, and I went to find sustenance. I can't remember when my special hairball-eliminating formula had tasted so good. As I lifted the tender morsels lovingly into my mouth, I closed my eyes and sighed in gratified pleasure. I really was happy to still be alive.

And, surprisingly, I was happy to see Maggie as she wandered up to me while I drained the water glass the Mrs. had placed lovingly on the floor.

Maggie took a few schleps schleps out of her own bowl, the errant droplets flying in my direction. Which is why I never drink from a container sitting on the floor, but the thought of a dehydration-induced death created a sudden desperation for this drink.

She stopped schlepping and turned to me. "Where have you been?"

"The Master locked me in that steel box in the back room."

She shuddered. "On purpose? You never get punished."

I paused mid-lick and thought for a moment. She was right, I never did get punished. But I also never committed any crime that would earn punishment, for everything I did was wonderful. Or I was smart enough not to get caught doing something that would incite The Master. Poor Maggie, though, was always in trouble. Her naughty times, like when she followed the Mrs. out into the front yard and took off running down the street, would always infuriate her mistress.

When she would eventually come home, she would receive a loud scolding of *"Bad dog!"* That title would follow any number of improper behaviors such as her living room carpet "accidents." I fail to see why the Mrs. called them accidents when they were anything but. They should have been called intentionals.

"I don't know if The Master shut me in there on purpose or not," I replied, "but if it had been intentional, it wasn't because he was punishing me."

"Then why did he shut the door?" she asked, perplexed.

"That I don't have an answer to." And I didn't. Why he failed to note my presence in the safe or look harder for me at bedtime was a quandary I would have to ruminate on after I'd had a nap in a safe location.

"It was kind of lonely last night without you," she admitted.

I felt truly touched. I would have replied with some sentimental rubbish, but we cats don't go out for such expressions of sentimentality. Once we start down that path, the spotlight no longer shines solely for us, and what would be the purpose of that? But still, I felt touched just the same.

"You must be really tired," she continued. "I was just going to take a nap, but I thought I'd let you pick which bed you wanted to sleep in first. Then I'll take the other one."

Now I felt doubly touched. She had to be the perfect example of how a dog should treat a cat. The animosity that exists between dogs and cats would be nonexistent if they gave us preferential treatment and kind consideration all of the time. As we of course deserve.

Chapter Sixteen

Canine Fashion Disasters

Humans have the wretched habit of dressing up their dogs in the most deplorable attire. From my perch atop the sofa I have observed these people while walking their dogs. Surely it must be for my amusement, as the silly canine at the end of the leash is often wearing a ludicrous looking coat draped from his shoulders to his haunches.

Personally, I thought the Chihuahua wearing the bright orange, green, and purple striped number to be the best in show. Why the very neon brightness of the outfit surely served to announce: make way, comical coat-wearing Chihuahua strutting his stuff.

Correction, he wasn't strutting, he was trotting. Chihuahuas have such short legs, they tend to trot as fast as their elfin legs will carry them behind a master dragging the senseless idiot down the street.

Once I glimpsed a poodle and her mistress wearing matching pink tracksuits. Such a farce, I tell you, as the little white hairball turned and caught my eye. She straightened and gave me her smartest look while I regarded her to be incredibly stupid for allowing the dressing up to take place at all.

And, lest I forget to mention, the embarrassing cone-shaped accoutrement I witnessed one retriever wearing around its neck. I cannot imagine strutting around the neighborhood wearing that device. If it hadn't been a dog, I would have felt embarrassed for the poor guy. But it was a dog after all, so I sneered in derision instead. Make no dog bones about it, all of us in the animal kingdom know what has taken place to cause the family pet to wear *the cone*. Let's see, how shall I describe this without offending someone with delicate sensibilities? I will just say some things that used to dangle from the posterior end have been removed in the hopes that Rover will no longer want to pursue Fifi, and stay home and enjoy companionable evenings with the family instead. Have you ever heard a Basset Hound howl at the moon in lovesick misery? Night after night the racket continues until I'm about ready to go over to the neighbors and give him something to howl about.

His owners must have been fed up with the howling at all hours, too. Hence the trip to the place that smells like fear, canine urine, and death. Snip, snip, and home he returned wearing the cone of shame until the snipped area had properly healed. And once the cone had been removed and the hound had returned to his normal half-witted self, no more howling at the moon in lovesick misery.

Dogs and their owners look utterly absurd in their dog-walking vestments. And I use the word "dogs" very liberally, for you will never witness an owner walking a cat on a leash. Such an idea is absolutely ludicrous, as we cats roam freely whenever and wherever we choose.

I'LL TELL YOU WHAT I THINK

All this talk of dog costumes has reminded me of Maggie. The time of year had arrived when the big tree appeared in the living room, and the Mrs. had the idea of purchasing a coat for Maggie. And not just any coat mind you, for this one was red and green accompanied by a little hat with a white ball on the end of it. Now the hat might perhaps be useful if I could manage to detach the ball and commence a good game of paw-bat, paw-bat. I envisioned myself having quite a go with it across the shiny wood floors, but as for envisioning Maggie wearing it, well, no, I certainly could *not* envision the poor thing in it.

For of late she had become a little absentminded, and I was afraid she would too easily allow herself to participate in the charade.

"What is that?" The Master queried.

The Mrs. removed the dreadful specimens from her shopping bag and held it up for him to admire. *"It's a Santa coat and matching hat. Isn't it great?"*

Too late I realized The Master's keen interest spelled trouble for our family canine. With a gleam in his eye, he seized the hat and placed it atop Maggie's head.

"No, you're putting it on wrong," the Mrs. corrected. She reached inside the hat, removed a strap, and laced it about Maggie's chin.

"That's so it will stay on," she said, stating the obvious.

Maggie began to shiver, and for once I wholeheartedly agreed with her body language. She might be starting to lose her kibbles, but she still had the sense to understand how lamentable this situation appeared. Whoever this Santa was, surely even he would object to this preposterous hat.

The hat drooped forward, depositing the white ball directly into Maggie's eye. She put her head down and lifted her paw to remove it from her head.

The Mrs. removed the white ball from Maggie's eye and reached to straighten the hat. *"No, Maggie!"* she directed.

She stood back and admired her little dog. *"Isn't she cute?"*

The Master gave a derisive snort. *"She looks like a rat in a hat."*

The Mrs. looked wounded. *"She does not! I think she looks adorable."*

Adorable my paw, she looked anything but. Maggie turned to look at me and sent me a bit of telepathic communication which I interpreted as help, how do I get out of this? I raised my whiskers, gave her a pointed look, and communicated back: I think you're going to have to play along, as the Mrs. tends to be rather insistent when she thinks something looks adorable.

I slunk away to the top of the stairs in case she had a matching cat costume hiding in the bag. I could just picture us standing side by side, resplendent in all our shame as the motley crew arrived for the holiday festivities. Perhaps she wanted us to serve the guests with trays balanced on our backs. "Can I offer you an aperitif before dinner?" I would ask. "A cocktail perchance featuring my own special recipe of pureed fish and liver? Or I also have an excellent wine with some resplendent bits of chopped gizzard."

The Mrs. picked up the coat and secured it lovingly on Maggie's body. *"This is so great!"* she said with delight. I debated on whether she thought Maggie looking foolish was great, or the fact that she had managed to snag such a disastrous fashion statement for her little one to model. *"Our guests will think you look so cute!"*

The hat slid unceremoniously from Maggie's head, landing askew over her ear and obscuring one eye. The Mrs. straightened it back up only to have it pitch forward over her entire face.

"I was afraid of this," she said. *"But not to worry, I planned for contingencies. If I am anything, I am efficient."*

She reached into the bag (was there no end to the dastardly nasties hiding inside?) and removed—oh no, it couldn't be. Yes, it was: a set of miniature reindeer antlers. She removed the hat, then placed the offensive brown ornaments atop Maggie's head, adjusted them, and affixed the long gripper apparatuses behind her ears. Well, that's what they were supposed to do, anyway, but whoever managed to get a dog to pose for the picture on the front of the bag must have been a genius. Either that, or they bribed the dog with an entire rack of ribs if he would stand at attention and pose fetchingly for the camera.

The antlers immediately pitched forward as Maggie bent her head to the ground and reached to paw them off.

"No, Maggie." the Mrs. instructed once again. *"Leave them alone."*

At this point I hoped the guests would arrive soon so as to be done with this charade of festive holiday attire. Knowing the Mrs., once the visitors showered her with the necessary oohs and ahs at the cuteness of her little one, she would disappear into the kitchen with her usual air of efficiency, and Maggie could relieve herself of this unwanted baggage.

The Mrs. reached down and pushed the antlers back into place. *"There, don't they look adorable?"*

The Master's eyes crinkled in mischievous merriment as he studied the obnoxious horns and pointed his finger at Maggie, his indication that she was to remain frozen in place and not move a muscle. He had spent long hours perfecting this technique over the years, and good-natured Maggie had gone along with it. Many's the time he sat her up against the sofa cushions with his finger cocked at her as he tsk-tsked and she tried her best to remain motionless for as long as possible until she would slowly start to sag sideways in a heap upon the cushions.

"*Ut-ut-ut!*" he would remonstrate as he reached to center her body back against the sofa and commenced the finger pointing once again. This game (on his part, not hers) would continue until he thankfully tired of posing her for "the finger."

Now this is something you would never see a human even think of attempting on a cat, for we are far too intelligent to allow a human to think they could train us to sit or fetch or roll over. And why in the world would I want to pretend I was dead? When I think of dogs allowing their masters to "train" them in such a manner, I can only shake my head in befuddlement. All of this nonsense for a doggie treat?

We felines have it figured out. All we have to do is turn our noses up at whatever treat our owners try to give us, while they keep increasing the many and resplendent offerings, until we are presented with the very best the world has to offer. And with no rolling over or speaking on command.

Maggie did her best to remain motionless, but it did not stop the antlers from pitching forward once again. She shook her head and sent them flying across the floor. The doorbell rang. Maggie began barking while the Mrs. retrieved the offensive antlers and hurriedly affixed them back on top of her head.

She opened the door, and the small people ran in followed by their parents. *"Oh, look at Maggie!"* they cried.

"Doesn't she look cute?" the Mrs. exclaimed as the antlers pitched forward. She bent down and scooped Maggie up into her arms. With one hand under her belly and the other on the antlers, she managed to present a picture of adorability while the rest of the family piled into the house and – right on cue – elicited the predictable oohs and ahs.

Maggie hung her head in shame, and I shook my head at the entire farce humans have created for their pets. If I ever see the Mrs. reach into another bag as she's reaching for me, my disappearing act will be so incredibly impressive, the relatives will have something even more extraordinary to ooh and ah about.

Chapter Seventeen

A Second Cracking

Time went by with more dining alfresco on warm summer evenings and indoor amusements during the cold months. I had grown quite fond of Maggie. I wouldn't call her a best friend as I am a loner and don't really care for company, but I could say I actually liked her. It must have been that bonding we participated in during the Mrs.' time of sadness. And the fact that she, a dog, actually took my advice and began to turn her countenance out instead of in. Such a relief, for I don't know how much longer I could endure her pathetic sad face and I-want-the-Mrs.-to-love-me attitude.

I didn't even feel resentment toward her when The Master and Mrs. would go away and ship me off to a boarding place called Sir Barkalot for dogs and cats. Maggie, on the other hand, would get a special pickup from one of the freeloading relatives and then be carted off to live with them for a while. I've heard these relatives discuss how they made her a special bed and fed her special treats. Really, if I weren't such a charitable soul, I would be absolutely angry at Maggie for getting the better end of the deal when I had to endure being locked away at the "camp" with other cats. Such an insulting experience. Here we were, thrown together in two rooms and expected to suddenly be "howdy neighbor!" friends.

There were a variety of perches and beds to choose from, but who could sleep in a place that smelled of so many others who had come from who knows where? And the food! Community bowls of victuals and water. Didn't the Mrs. instruct them I only drink from real glass that is kept up high where I can jump up and sample it? I *never* drink from a community bowl sitting on the ground as if I were a common alley cat. Well, all I can say is I'm thankful I like to sleep a lot, because I had no other alternative than to crawl in one of those smelly beds, close my eyes, and hope my family would arrive soon to collect me.

Although, who could sleep with nonstop barking day and night? The other part of the place was a camp for dogs, large and small, ugly and uglier, that did nothing but bark (hence the name). At least at home I only had to contend with Maggie's occasional bark—and Duke's when he came to visit, but I had learned to tune him out. An utter waste of my time to even feel annoyed at such a moron.

When I would return home from my "camp" the Mrs. would instruct me to *"go get the stink off."* Apparently I came home smelling like whatever they used to scrub the floor. Believe me, I was more than anxious to get the stink off, for I was covered with more than some odorous disinfectant as they called it. I was covered with every cat who had ever been in that place!

My usual method would be to first roll in the rich, brown dirt of The Master's flower beds, a move sure to elicit some loud complaint from him.

I'LL TELL YOU WHAT I THINK

"You're not coming in the house with that dirt all over you!"

And, predictably, the Mrs. would lovingly run and brush all the dirt off my coat so that I could be allowed inside. Then I would really go to work bathing myself from top to bottom until I was certain that stink had been eradicated completely.

Maggie would come home at the same time from her luxury boarding and we would greet each other with a friendly little nudge and settle into our beds upstairs. But as of late she seemed unable to remember who I was. The fur around her face had turned gray, her eyes seemed cloudy, and she behaved as if she didn't remember where she was, which had begun to present itself as a problem. Sadly, I knew Maggie's time on earth would soon come to an end.

She did, however, always know the Mrs. Recently when the Mrs. would pick her up though, she would stiffen and give a little inward groan as if in pain.

I heard the Mrs. discussing it with The Master. *"At times she acts like a puppy, running up and down the stairs, but at other times she walks around like she doesn't know who she is."*

Our conversations had become less frequent over time as Maggie seemed to lapse into a world of her own. Then we eventually ceased conversing altogether. She had become a shell of a dog, lost to everyone but her mistress.

One afternoon The Master, Mrs., and a relative were in the kitchen discussing the situation. Water started leaking from the Mrs.' eyes as she said, *"I don't know if I can do this. Do you really think it's time?"*

The relative said, *"Look at Maggie. She doesn't know who she is anymore. Haven't you noticed how she seems to be in pain all the time?"*

The Mrs. put her hand up to her face and studied the one she loved best. A flicker of understanding entered her eyes as she seemed to view her little darling in a new light. Perhaps she had been in denial about how dire the situation had become. She tenderly picked Maggie up and left the house.

When the Mrs. returned, she was alone.

I didn't know where she had taken Maggie. I can only guess it must have been that awful place that smelled like fear, canine urine, and death, and I knew for certain she would never be coming back.

And for the second time my heart cracked, along with the Mrs.' She was grief-stricken afresh, but in a different way than the great sadness, the death of her sister. She understood, as we all do, that there comes a time when you have to say goodbye to the family pet. Our time on earth is limited, and we give it our all to be a part of the family while we are here.

And with this second cracking of my heart, I committed then and there to do my best to help the Mrs. through Maggie's departure, because she no longer had her little dog to render comfort.

I found the Mrs. sitting on the sofa, and I hopped into her lap. Her voice broke as she put her arms around me and said, *"Oh, Thor, you're such a comfort."*

And at that moment I became her little darling. I became the one she loved best, as she began to tell me frequently from that point on. I threw myself into that role wholeheartedly. How marvelous it felt to curl up on her legs while she watched TV or slept. What comfort, what joy they felt to have me around.

I'LL TELL YOU WHAT I THINK

When the Mrs. would come home from an outing she would remark, "*Maggie's presence is so strong. I can feel her everywhere.*"

And so did I. At times I would start up the stairs and feel her bounding up behind me. I would pause and turn around only to find she wasn't really there. I knew that, but it certainly *felt* like it. The Mrs. had been right, we felt her presence everywhere.

Especially when I went upstairs to search for a good napping spot. I could swear she was asleep in one of our beds, so I couldn't bring myself to lie in either one. After enough time had passed and the Mrs. understood I would never use either one of them again, she removed them from the bedroom.

After a while the Mrs. presented me with a brand new bed. Such rapture, such wonder I never had known. This new bed was mine, all mine, and smelled only of me. And to prove she loved me, she had the consideration to move it in front of the furnace vent. Heaven, pure heaven. Do you want to know the best part of all? She calls me her little buddy.

AND SO, I HAVE COME to the denouement in my memoir. If you have paid close attention, you will begin jumping about for joy as you learn to more fully embrace life (not something *I* would do, but it made Maggie happier), know how to bend others to your will and, no matter the circumstances, understand how to look cool at all costs. Even if it requires a good lick to your nether regions in a show of nonchalance.

The night is warm with the wonderful smells of summer drifting along the breeze. I am lying on the sun-warmed bricks surrounding the pool while The Master, the Mrs. and extended freeloaders consume great quantities of their expertly crafted fare.

I am the master of my kingdom, and life is good. And as I am lying with my eyes closed in contentment and just drifting off to sleep, I hear a commotion arise from somewhere in the back corner of the yard. I think I will go and find out what it is.

www.ingramcontent.com/pod-product-compliance
Lightning Source LLC
Chambersburg PA
CBHW051831040426
42447CB00006B/472